C0-BLE-549

WHAT THE BIBLE SAYS ABOUT DEALING WITH DIFFICULT TIMES

BY CRISWELL FREEMAN

Contents

A MESSAGE TO READERS

We know that all things work together
for the good of those who love God:
those who are called according to His purpose.

ROMANS 8:28 HCSB

God's Word promises that all things work together for the good of those who love Him. Yet sometimes we encounter situations that seem so troubling that we simply cannot comprehend how those events might be a part of God's plan for our lives. We experience difficult times—perhaps the loss of money or health; perhaps divorce, job loss, or a broken personal relationship—and we honestly wonder if recovery is possible. But with God, all things are possible.

The Christian faith, as communicated through the words of the Holy Bible, is a healing faith. It offers comfort in times of trouble, courage instead of fear, and hope instead of hopelessness. God's Word contains promises that you can depend on and wisdom that you can trust in both good times and hard times.

If you are experiencing the pain of a recent setback, or if you are still mourning a loss from long ago, this book is intended to help. When you weave God's message into the fabric of your day, you'll quickly discover that God's Word has the power to change everything, including you.

WHAT THE
BIBLE
SAYS ABOUT
DEALING
WITH
DIFFICULT
TIMES

SMITH
FREEMAN
Publishing

What the Bible Says about Dealing with Difficult Times
by Criswell Freeman

©2021 Smith Freeman Publishing

Bible verses were taken from the following translations:

Scripture quotations marked HCSB are taken from the Holman Christian Standard Bible®, Used by Permission HCSB © 1999, 2000, 2002, 2003, 2009 Holman Bible Publishers. Holman Christian Standard Bible®, Holman CSB®, and HCSB® are federally registered trademarks of Holman Bible Publishers.

Scripture quotations marked (KJV) are from the King James Version. Public domain.

Scripture quotations marked MSG are taken from THE MESSAGE, copyright © 1993, 2002, 2018 by Eugene H. Peterson. Used by permission of NavPress. All rights reserved. Represented by Tyndale House Publishers, a Division of Tyndale House Ministries.

Scripture quotations marked (NASB) are from the New American Standard Bible® (NASB), Copyright © 1960, 1962, 1963,1968, 1971, 1972, 1973, 1975, 1977, 1995 by The Lockman Foundation. Used by permission. www.Lockman.org.

Scripture quotations marked (NCV) are taken from the New Century Version®. Copyright © 2005 by Thomas Nelson. Used by permission. All rights reserved.

Scripture quotations marked (NIV) are taken from the Holy Bible, New International Version®, NIV®. Copyright © 1973, 1978, 1984, 2011 by Biblica, Inc.™ Used by permission of Zondervan. All rights reserved worldwide. www.zondervan.com The "NIV" and "New International Version" are trademarks registered in the United States Patent and Trademark Office by Biblica, Inc.™

Scripture quotations marked (NKJV) are taken from the New King James Version®. Copyright © 1982 by Thomas Nelson. Used by permission. All rights reserved.

Scripture quotations marked (NLT) are taken from the Holy Bible, New Living Translation, copyright © 1996, 2004, 2015 by Tyndale House Foundation. Used by permission of Tyndale House Publishers, a Division of Tyndale House Ministries, Carol Stream, Illinois 60188. All rights reserved.

Cover design by Kim Russell | Wahoo Designs

ISBN: 978-1-7349737-6-1

Adversity is not meant to be feared; it is meant to be worked through. If this text assists you, even in a small way, as you move through and beyond your own difficult times, this book will have served its purpose. May the Lord bless you and keep you, and may He place His hand upon your heart today, tomorrow, and forever.

12 ESSENTIAL STEPS FOR DEALING WITH DIFFICULT TIMES

When Times Are Tough, Remember That God Is Still in Control and You Are Still Protected. Tough times are temporary, but God's love is eternal. So if your life seems to be spinning out of control, remind yourself that the Lord is always in control and that He is always your Shepherd.

Keep Things in Perspective. During difficult times, it's easy to lose perspective and it's easy to magnify the size of your problems—easy, but wrong. So if you've encountered difficult circumstances, ask the Lord to help you keep things in perspective. After all, the challenges that seem monumental today may not seem nearly as daunting next week or next month or next year.

Never Abandon Hope. During difficult days, hope can be a scarce commodity, so if you're experiencing difficult times, you'll be wise to start spending more time with God. If you do your part, the Lord will do His part. Knowing that God is on your side will give you confidence, and God's Word will be a constant reminder that you should never be afraid to hope—or to ask—for a miracle.

Keep Praying for God's Guidance. If you want God's guidance, ask for it. When you pray for guidance, the Lord will give it. He will guide your steps if you let Him; your task, simply put, is to study, to pray, to listen, to learn, and to follow.

Seek Advice from Friends and Mentors. During difficult times, don't hesitate to reach out for support from friends, family members, mentors, or your pastor. Proverbs 1:5 makes it clear: "A wise man will hear and increase learning, and a man of understanding will attain wise counsel" (NKJV).

Make Peace with Your Past. The past is past, so don't invest all your energy there. If you're focused on the past, change your focus. If you're living in the past, ask the Lord to help you trust Him more so you can accept your present circumstances and move on with your life.

When You Experience a Major Life-altering Change or a Significant Loss, Express Your Feelings Honestly. If you're experiencing a life-changing event, or if you're recovering from a recent disappointment, don't keep everything bottled up inside. Instead, talk honestly and openly with people you can trust. And while you're at it, remember that God promises to heal the brokenhearted. In time, He will heal your heart and dry your tears if you let Him. So if you haven't already allowed Him to begin His healing process, today is a perfect day to start.

Avoid the Pitfalls of Procrastination. Procrastination breeds worry; worry breeds anxiety; anxiety breeds fear; fear breeds more procrastination, and the cycle continues. If you're constantly putting off until tomorrow what should be done today, you're actually manufacturing things to worry about. A far better strategy is undoubtedly this: tackle today's problems *today* so that you don't have to worry about them *tomorrow*.

Forgive Everybody. Hate and peace cannot coexist in the same human heart. God's Word makes it clear that if you want to experience the peace that passes all understanding—His peace—then you must learn how to forgive people and move on with your life. So the sooner you forgive everybody—including yourself—the sooner you'll begin feeling better about yourself and your circumstances.

Get Plenty of Rest. Most adults need about eight hours of sleep each night. If you're constantly depriving yourself of much-needed sleep, you may be harming your overall health while manufacturing needless stress and anxiety. So if you've acquired the habit of staying up late and robbing yourself of sleep, it's time to establish a new (and better) habit by turning off your devices and going to bed at a reasonable hour. But what if you're simply too anxious or too worried to fall asleep or to stay asleep? If you can't sleep, talk with your physician about your sleeping patterns, your situation, your habits, and your emotional state. You can establish better sleeping habits—and you should—because you need a good night's sleep to think clearly and realistically about your life, your blessings, your plans, and your future.

Be Patient, Be Satisfied with Incremental Progress, and Don't Give Up. Persistence is power; patience is wisdom; and progress, no matter how small, is still progress. So if you're working hard to resolve your challenges, keep working, keep praying, and stay hopeful. Remember that you and God, working together, can accomplish great things because nothing is impossible for Him.

If Your Emotions—or the Emotions of Someone You Love— Begin to Spiral Out of Control, Seek Professional Help Immediately. Small emotional swings are an inevitable part of everyday life. But dramatic emotional swings—such as intense feelings of anxiety, despair, panic, or fear—are dangerous. So don't ever be embarrassed to seek professional help if you're feeling overwhelmed by your circumstances. And if someone you trust suggests that you should seek counseling, take that advice to heart. Mental health professionals have numerous tools at their disposal to help you deal with emotional swings, depression, and anxiety disorders. Since help is available, you should ask for it as soon as you detect a problem.

1

GOD WILL HELP YOU DEAL WITH DIFFICULT TIMES

What the Bible Says

*He heals the brokenhearted
and binds up their wounds.*

PSALM 147:3 HCSB

From time to time, all of us encounter difficult times. None of us are exempt from occasional setbacks, disappointments, failures, and hardships. When tough times arrive, we may be forced to rearrange our plans and our priorities, but even on our darkest days, we should remember that God's love remains constant. And we must never forget that the Lord intends for us to use our setbacks as stepping stones on the path to a better life.

When times are tough, the words of Jesus offer us comfort. The Son of God said, "These things I have spoken to you, that in Me you may have peace. In the world you will have tribulation; but be of good cheer, I have overcome the world" (John 16:33 NKJV). And Psalm 145 promises, "The LORD is near to all who call on him, to all who call on him in truth. He fulfills the desires of those who fear him; he hears their cry and saves them" (v. 18–19 NIV).

Life is a tapestry of good days and difficult days, with good days predominating. During the good days, we are tempted to take our blessings for granted (a temptation that we must resist). But during life's difficult days, we discover precisely what we're made of. And more importantly, we discover what our faith is made of.

Throughout the seasons of life, we occasionally experience life-altering personal losses that leave us breathless. Thankfully, God has promised that He will never desert us. And the Lord always keeps His promises.

MORE THOUGHTS ABOUT DEALING WITH DIFFICULT TIMES

If God sends us on stony paths,
He provides strong shoes.
CORRIE TEN BOOM

God will not permit any troubles to come upon
us unless He has a specific plan by which great
blessing can come out of the difficulty.
PETER MARSHALL

Every misfortune, every failure, every loss may
be transformed. God has the power
to transform all misfortunes into "God-sends."
LETTIE COWMAN

As we wait on God, He helps us use the winds
of adversity to soar above our problems.
As the Bible says, "Those who wait on the LORD . . .
shall mount up with wings like eagles."
BILLY GRAHAM

Often the trials we mourn are really
gateways into the good things we long for.
HANNAH WHITALL SMITH

MORE FROM GOD'S WORD

I called to the Lord in my distress; I called to my God. From His temple He heard my voice.

2 Samuel 22:7 HCSB

We are hard-pressed on every side, yet not crushed; we are perplexed, but not in despair.

2 Corinthians 4:8 NKJV

God blesses those who patiently endure testing. Afterward they will receive the crown of life that God has promised to those who love him.

James 1:12 NLT

REMEMBER THIS

Difficult times are simply opportunities to trust God completely and to find strength in Him. And remember that hard times can also be times of intense personal growth.

A TIMELY TIP

If you're experiencing tough times, don't hit the panic button and don't keep everything bottled up inside. Instead, talk things over with people you can really trust. A second opinion (or for that matter, a third, fourth, or fifth opinion) is usually helpful. So if your troubles seem overwhelming, don't be afraid or embarrassed to ask for help.

2
PUT GOD FIRST

WHAT THE BIBLE SAYS

*But seek first the kingdom of God
and His righteousness,
and all these things will be provided for you.*
MATTHEW 6:33 HCSB

When God handed down the Ten Commandments, He made it abundantly clear that we must have no other gods before Him. Yet the world tempts us to do otherwise. The world is a noisy, distracting place, a place that offers countless temptations and dangers. The world seems to cry, "Worship me with your time, your money, your energy, your thoughts, and your life!" But if we are wise, we won't fall prey to that temptation.

As you think about the nature of your relationship with the Lord, remember this: You will always have some type of relationship with Him. The question is not *if* you will have a relationship with Him; the burning question is whether that relationship will be one that seeks to honor Him . . . or not.

Are you willing to place God first in your life? And are you willing to welcome God's Son into your heart? Unless you can honestly answer these questions with a resounding yes, then your relationship with the Lord isn't what it could be or should be. Thankfully, God is always available, He's always ready to forgive, and He's waiting to hear from you now. The rest, of course, is up to you.

MORE THOUGHTS ABOUT
PUTTING GOD FIRST

To God be the glory, great things He hath done;
So loved He the world that He gave us His Son.

FANNY CROSBY

Worship in the truest sense takes place
only when our full attention is on God—
His glory, majesty, love, and compassion.

BILLY GRAHAM

One with God is a majority.

BILLY GRAHAM

When all else is gone,
God is still left. Nothing changes Him.

HANNAH WHITALL SMITH

We become whatever
we are committed to.

RICK WARREN

God's purpose for us is that we ought to be
conformed to the image of His Son.

BILLY GRAHAM

MORE FROM GOD'S WORD

You shall have no other gods before Me.
Exodus 20:3 NKJV

Therefore, whether you eat or drink,
or whatever you do,
do all to the glory of God.
1 Corinthians 10:31 NKJV

For this is the love of God,
that we keep His commandments.
And His commandments are not burdensome.
1 John 5:3 NKJV

REMEMBER THIS

God deserves first place in your heart, and you deserve the experience of putting Him there.

A TIMELY TIP

Think about your priorities. Are you *really* putting God first in your life, or are you putting other things—things like possessions, hobbies, media, or personal status—ahead of your relationship with the Father? If, after honest self-evaluation, you believe that your priorities are misaligned, think of at least three things you can do today to put God where He belongs: in first place.

3

THE LORD CAN GIVE YOU THE COURAGE AND THE STRENGTH TO MEET ANY CHALLENGE

WHAT THE BIBLE SAYS

Be strong and courageous, and do the work.
Do not be afraid or discouraged,
for the LORD God, my God, is with you.
1 CHRONICLES 28:20 NIV

Every life (including yours) is an unfolding series of events: some fabulous, some not so fabulous, and some downright disheartening. When you reach the mountaintops of life, praising God is easy. But when the storm clouds form overhead, your faith can be tested, sometimes to the breaking point. When your faith is being tested, you can take comfort in this fact: wherever you find yourself, whether at the top of the mountain or the depths of the valley, God is there, and because He cares for you, you can live courageously.

Christians have every reason to be courageous. After all, the ultimate battle has already been fought and won on the cross at Calvary. But even dedicated followers of Christ may become discouraged by the inevitable disappointments and tragedies that occur in the lives of believers and nonbelievers alike.

The next time you find your courage tested to the limit, remember that God is as near as your next breath, and remember that He is your shield and your strength. He is your protector and your deliverer. Call upon Him in your hour of need and then be comforted. Whatever your challenge, whatever your trouble, God can handle it. And will.

MORE THOUGHTS ABOUT COURAGE

*Do not let Satan deceive you into being
afraid of God's plans for your life.*
R. A. TORREY

*Courage is not simply one of the virtues,
but the form of every virtue at the testing point.*
C. S. LEWIS

*Just as courage is faith in good,
so discouragement is faith in evil,
and, while courage opens the door to good,
discouragement opens it to evil.*
HANNAH WHITALL SMITH

*In my experience, God rarely makes
our fear disappear. Instead, He asks us
to be strong and take courage.*
BRUCE WILKINSON

*Every difficult task that comes across your path—
every one that you would rather not do, that will
take the most effort, cause the most pain, and be
the greatest struggle—brings a blessing with it.*
LETTIE COWMAN

*Take courage. We walk in the wilderness today
and in the Promised Land tomorrow.*

D. L. MOODY

MORE FROM GOD'S WORD

*For God has not given us a spirit of fearfulness,
but one of power, love, and sound judgment.*

2 TIMOTHY 1:7 HCSB

*Be on guard. Stand firm in the faith.
Be courageous. Be strong.*

1 CORINTHIANS 16:13 NLT

*Behold, God is my salvation;
I will trust, and not be afraid.*

ISAIAH 12:2 KJV

REMEMBER THIS

If you trust God completely—and if you're a disciple of His Son—you have every reason on earth—and in heaven—to live courageously.

A TIMELY TIP

Is your courage being tested today? If so, cling tightly to God's promises, and pray. The Lord can give you the strength to meet any challenge, and that's exactly what you should ask Him to do right now.

4

BECAUSE GOD IS FAITHFUL, YOU CAN ALWAYS HAVE HOPE

WHAT THE BIBLE SAYS

Let us hold fast the confession of our hope without wavering, for He who promised is faithful.
HEBREWS 10:23 NASB

On the darkest days of our lives, we may be confronted with an illusion that seems very real indeed: the illusion of hopelessness. Try though we might, we simply can't envision a solution to our problems. Despite God's promises, despite Christ's love, and despite our many blessings, we may abandon hope. These dark days can be dangerous times for us and for our loved ones.

If you find yourself falling into the spiritual traps of worry and discouragement, seek the encouraging words of fellow Christians, and the healing touch of God's only begotten Son. After all, it was Christ who promised, "These things I have spoken unto you, that in me ye might have peace. In the world ye shall have tribulation: but be of good cheer; I have overcome the world" (John 16:33 KJV).

Can you summon the faith to trust God in good times and hard times? If you can, you will be blessed. And once you've made the decision to trust God completely, it's time to get busy. The willingness to take action—even if the outcome of that action is uncertain—is an effective way to combat hopelessness. When you decide to roll up your sleeves and begin solving your own problems, you'll feel empowered, and you will inevitably begin to see the first real glimmer of hope.

The American publisher Cyrus Curtis had the following advice. He said, "Believe in the Lord and He will do half the work—the last half." So today and every day, ask God for these things: clear perspective, mountain-moving faith, and the courage to do what needs to be done. After all, no challenge is too big for God—not even yours.

MORE THOUGHTS ABOUT HOPE

Without the certainty of His resurrection, we would come to the end of this life without hope, with nothing to anticipate except despair and doubt. But because He lives, we rejoice, knowing soon we will meet our Savior face to face, and the troubles and trials of this world will be behind us.

BILL BRIGHT

Down through the centuries in times of trouble and trial, God has brought courage to the hearts of those who love Him. The Bible is filled with assurances of God's help and comfort in every kind of trouble which might cause fears to arise in the human heart. You can look ahead with promise, hope, and joy.

BILLY GRAHAM

Faith looks back and draws courage; hope looks ahead and keeps desire alive.

JOHN ELDREDGE

If your hopes are being disappointed just now,
it means that they are being purified.

OSWALD CHAMBERS

MORE FROM GOD'S WORD

This hope we have as an anchor of the soul,
a hope both sure and steadfast.
HEBREWS 6:19 NASB

Hope deferred makes the heart sick.
PROVERBS 13:12 NKJV

Be strong and courageous,
all you who put your hope in the LORD.
PSALM 31:24 HCSB

REMEMBER THIS

Because the Lord is on your side—and by your side—you should never lose hope. With God, all things are possible.

A TIMELY TIP

If you're experiencing hard times, you'll be wise to start spending more time with God. And if you do your part, the Lord will most certainly do His part. So never be afraid to hope—or to pray—for a miracle.

5

PATIENCE IS A POWERFUL TOOL FOR DEALING WITH DIFFICULT TIMES

WHAT THE BIBLE SAYS

The LORD is good to those who depend on him,
to those who search for him. So it is good
to wait quietly for salvation from the LORD.

LAMENTATIONS 3:25–26 NLT

The dictionary defines the word patience as "the ability to be calm, tolerant, and understanding." If that describes you, you can skip this chapter. But if you're like most of us, you'd better keep reading. For most of us, patience is a hard thing to master. Why? Because we have lots of things we want, and we know precisely when we want them: *now.* But our Father in heaven may have other plans for us. So the Bible teaches us to wait patiently for the things that the Lord has in store for us, even when waiting is difficult.

We live in an imperfect world inhabited by imperfect people. Sometimes we inherit troubles from others, and sometimes we create troubles for ourselves. Sometimes we see other people "moving ahead" in the world, and we want to move ahead with them, and we become impatient with ourselves, with our circumstances, and even with our Creator.

Patience is not only a virtue; it is also the price we pay for being responsible adults. And that's as it should be. After all, think how patient our heavenly Father has been with us.

WHEN WE'RE ENDURING TOUGH TIMES, WE MUST TRUST GOD'S TIMING

He has made everything appropriate in its time.
He has also put eternity in their hearts,
but man cannot discover the work
God has done from beginning to end.

ECCLESIASTES 3:11 HCSB

Sometimes the hardest thing to do is to wait. This is especially true when times are tough. When life throws us a curveball, we're naturally in a hurry for God to repair things immediately, if not sooner! But God's plan does not always unfold in the way that we would like or at the time of our own choosing. Our task—as thoughtful men and women who trust in a benevolent, all-knowing Father—is to wait patiently for God to reveal Himself.

Are you experiencing difficult times? If so, don't give up, don't give in, and don't stop talking to God. He will answer your prayers at the proper time. Your job is to keep working—and praying—until He does.

Lettie Cowman said, "We often hear about waiting on God, which actually means that He is waiting until we are ready.

There is another side, however. When we wait for God, we are waiting until He is ready.

MORE THOUGHTS ABOUT PATIENCE

Frustration is not the will of God.
There is time to do anything and everything
that God wants us to do.

ELISABETH ELLIOT

Patience is the companion of wisdom.

ST. AUGUSTINE

By His wisdom, He orders His delays
so that they prove to be
far better than our hurries.

C. H. SPURGEON

As we wait on God, He helps us use
the winds of adversity to soar above our problems.
As the Bible says, "Those who wait on the LORD . . .
shall mount up with wings like eagles."

BILLY GRAHAM

You can't step in front of God
and not get in trouble. When He says,
"Go three steps," don't go four.

CHARLES STANLEY

To wait upon God is the perfection of activity.

OSWALD CHAMBERS

MORE FROM GOD'S WORD

A person's wisdom yields patience;
it is to one's glory to overlook an offense.
PROVERBS 19:11 NIV

Patience of spirit is better than
haughtiness of spirit.
ECCLESIASTES 7:8 NASB

Better to be patient than powerful;
better to have self-control
than to conquer a city.
PROVERBS 16:32 NLT

REMEMBER THIS

The best things in life seldom happen overnight; they usually take time. Henry Blackaby wrote, "The grass that is here today and gone tomorrow does not require much time to mature. A big oak tree that lasts for generations requires much more time to grow and mature. God is concerned about your life through eternity. Allow Him to take all the time He needs to shape you for His purposes. Larger assignments will require longer periods of preparation." How true.

A TIMELY TIP

If you'd like to become a more patient person, pray about it. God can help you do things that you can't do by yourself.

6

GOD GUIDES US THROUGH DIFFICULT TIMES

WHAT THE BIBLE SAYS

Trust in the Lord with all your heart,
and lean not on your own understanding;
in all your ways acknowledge Him,
and He shall direct your paths.

PROVERBS 3:5–6 NKJV

When we ask for God's guidance, with our hearts and minds open to His direction, He will lead us along a path of His choosing. But for many of us, listening to the Lord is hard. We have so many things we want, and so many needs to pray for, that we spend far more time talking at God than we do listening to Him.

Corrie ten Boom observed, "God's guidance is even more important than common sense. I can declare that the deepest darkness is outshone by the light of Jesus." These words remind us that life is best lived when we seek the Lord's direction early and often.

Our Father has many ways to make Himself known. Our challenge is to make ourselves open to His instruction. So if you're unsure of your next step, trust God's promises and talk to Him often. When you do, He'll guide your steps today, tomorrow, and forever.

MORE THOUGHTS ABOUT GOD'S GUIDANCE

*It's important that you keep asking God
to show you what He wants you to do.
If you don't ask, you won't know.*

STORMIE OMARTIAN

*As you walk through the valley of the unknown,
you will find the footprints of Jesus
both in front of you and beside you.*

CHARLES STANLEY

*God never leads us to do anything
that is contrary to the Bible.*

BILLY GRAHAM

*When we are obedient,
God guides our steps and our stops.*

CORRIE TEN BOOM

*Are you serious about wanting God's guidance
to become a personal reality in your life? The
first step is to tell God that you know you can't
manage your own life; that you need His help.*

CATHERINE MARSHALL

*The will of God will never take us where
the grace of God cannot sustain us.*

BILLY GRAHAM

MORE FROM GOD'S WORD

*The L*ORD *says, "I will guide you along*
the best pathway for your life.
I will advise you and watch over you."
PSALM 32:8 NLT

Teach me to do Your will, for You are my God;
Your Spirit is good.
Lead me in the land of uprightness.
PSALM 143:10 NKJV

*Shew me thy ways, O L*ORD; *teach me thy paths.*
Lead me in thy truth, and teach me:
for thou art the God of my salvation;
on thee do I wait all the day.
PSALM 25:4–5 KJV

REMEMBER THIS

God loves you and He wants you to follow in the footsteps of His Son. When you're following in Christ's footsteps, you're always on the right path.

A TIMELY TIP

If you're serious about receiving God's guidance, ask Him for it. When you pray for guidance, the Lord will give it (Luke 11:9). So ask.

7

NO PROBLEMS ARE TOO BIG FOR GOD

WHAT THE BIBLE SAYS

People who do what is right may have many problems, but the LORD will solve them all.

PSALM 34:19 NCV

Life is an adventure in problem solving. The question is not *whether* we will encounter problems; the real question is how we will choose to address them. When it comes to solving the challenges of everyday living, we often know precisely what needs to be done, but we may be slow in doing it—especially if what needs to be done is difficult. So we put off till tomorrow what should be done today.

As a person living here in the twenty-first century, you have your own set of challenges. As you face those challenges, you may be comforted by this fact: Trouble, of every kind, is temporary, but God's grace is eternal. And worries, of every kind, are temporary. But God's love is everlasting. The difficulties that concern you today will soon pass. God remains. And for every problem, He has a solution.

The words of Psalm 34 remind us that the Lord solves problems for "people who do what is right." And usually, doing "what is right" means doing the uncomfortable work of confronting our problems sooner rather than later. So with no further ado, let the problem solving begin. Now.

THE LORD CAN HELP YOUR RISE ABOVE DIFFICULT CIRCUMSTANCES

God is our protection and our strength.
He always helps in times of trouble.

PSALM 46:1 NCV

You've probably heard it said on many occasions, and perhaps you've even said it yourself: "I'm doing the best I can under the circumstances." But God has a better way. He wants you to live *above* your circumstances—and with His help, you can most certainly do it.

In Philippians, Paul stated that he could find happiness and fulfillment in any situation (Philippians 4:11). How? By turning his life and his future over to God. Even when he faced enormous difficulties, Paul found peace through God. So can you.

Charles Stanley observed, "Oftentimes God demonstrates His faithfulness in adversity by providing for us what we need to survive. He does not change our painful circumstances. He sustains us through them."

Today, make this important promise to yourself and to your Creator: Promise to rise far above your circumstances. You deserve no less, and neither, for that matter, does your heavenly Father.

MORE THOUGHTS ABOUT PROBLEM SOLVING

God is bigger than your problems. Whatever worries press upon you today, put them in God's hands and leave them there.

BILLY GRAHAM

*Every problem comes gift-wrapped in a package
that also contains a creative solution.
When you open the package that contains
the problem, the solution is there, too.
Your job is to accept both gifts.*

MARIE T. FREEMAN

*God has a purpose behind every problem.
He uses circumstances to develop our character.
In fact, He depends more on
circumstances to make us like Jesus
than He depends on our reading the Bible.*

RICK WARREN

Each problem is a God-appointed instructor.

CHARLES SWINDOLL

*We are all faced with a series of great opportunities,
brilliantly disguised as unsolvable problems.
Unsolvable without God's wisdom, that is.*

CHARLES SWINDOLL

Let God's promises shine on your problems.

CORRIE TEN BOOM

MORE FROM GOD'S WORD

*We are pressured in every way but not crushed;
we are perplexed but not in despair.*

2 CORINTHIANS 4:8 HCSB

Consider it a great joy, my brothers, whenever you experience various trials, knowing that the testing of your faith produces endurance. But endurance must do its complete work, so that you may be mature and complete, lacking nothing.

JAMES 1:2–4 HCSB

We also have joy with our troubles, because we know that these troubles produce patience. And patience produces character, and character produces hope.

ROMANS 5:3–4 NCV

REMEMBER THIS

Since problems don't usually fix themselves, you'll probably need to solve your own. And with God's help, you can.

A TIMELY TIP

Today, think about the wisdom of tackling your problems sooner rather than later. Remember that "this, too, will pass," but whatever "it" is will pass more quickly if you spend more time solving your problems and less time fretting about them.

8

WHEN TIMES ARE TOUGH, YOU MUST GUARD YOUR HEART AND YOUR THOUGHTS

WHAT THE BIBLE SAYS

*Guard your heart above all else,
for it is the source of life.*
PROVERBS 4:23 HCSB

Because we are human, we are always busy with our thoughts. We simply can't help ourselves. Our brains never shut off, and even while we're sleeping, we mull things over in our minds. The question is not if we will think; the question is how we will think and what we will think about.

Paul Valéry observed, "We hope vaguely but dread precisely." How true. All too often, we allow the worries of everyday life to overwhelm our thoughts and cloud our vision. What's needed is clearer perspective, renewed faith, and a different focus.

When we focus on the frustrations of today or the uncertainties of tomorrow, we rob ourselves of peace in the present moment. But when we direct our thoughts in more positive directions, we rid ourselves of the worries that have the power to tyrannize us.

The American poet Phoebe Cary observed, "All the great blessings of my life are present in my thoughts today." And her words apply to you. You will make your life better when you focus your thoughts on your blessings, not your misfortunes. So do yourself, your family, your friends, and your coworkers a favor: Learn to think optimistically about the world you live in and the life you lead. Then prepare yourself for the blessings that good thoughts inevitably bring.

UNDERSTANDING DEPRESSION

The sadness that accompanies any significant loss is an inescapable fact of life. Throughout our lives, all of us must endure the kinds of deep personal losses that leave us struggling to find hope. But in time, we move beyond our grief as the sadness gradually abates. Normal grief runs its course as the emotional pain slowly subsides, but clinical depression is different.

Depression is a physical and emotional condition that is, in most cases, treatable with medication and counseling. Depression is not a disease to be taken lightly. Left untreated, it presents real dangers to patients' physical health and to their emotional well-being. Thankfully, clinical depression is a highly treatable condition.

If you find yourself feeling blue, perhaps it's a logical reaction to the ups and downs of daily life. But if your feelings of sadness have lasted longer than you think they should—or if someone close to you fears that your sadness may have evolved into clinical depression—it's time to seek professional help.

If you're gripped by depression, God may seem far away. But He is not. The Lord is always available, always ready to send friends, family members, and healers to help you. Your job, simply put, is to be open to their advice and to accept the forms of treatment they recommend.

God's abundance is available to each of us. He offers His blessings, but He doesn't force them upon us. In John 10:10, Jesus promises, "I have come that they may have life, and that they may have it more abundantly" (NKJV). Depression is an illness that robs us of the joy and the peace that might otherwise be ours in Christ, so sufferers who wish to claim God's abundance are wise to seek medical intervention and counseling as soon as symptoms arise. Why? Because healing is available; it's effective; and it's part of God's plan.

MORE THOUGHTS ABOUT GUARDING YOUR THOUGHTS

Your life today is a result of your thinking yesterday. Your life tomorrow will be determined by what you think today.

JOHN MAXWELL

It is the thoughts and intents of the heart that shape a person's life.

JOHN ELDREDGE

The things we think are the things that feed our souls. If we think on pure and lovely things, we shall grow pure and lovely like them; and the converse is equally true.

HANNAH WHITALL SMITH

When you think on the powerful truths of Scripture, God uses His Word to change your way of thinking.

ELIZABETH GEORGE

The mind is like a clock that is constantly running down. It has to be wound up daily with good thoughts.

FULTON J. SHEEN

MORE FROM GOD'S WORD

Finally, brothers and sisters, whatever is true, whatever is noble, whatever is right, whatever is pure, whatever is lovely, whatever is admirable—if anything is excellent or praiseworthy—think about such things.
PHILIPPIANS 4:8 NIV

Set your mind on things above, not on things on the earth.
COLOSSIANS 3:2 NKJV

The peace of God, which surpasses all understanding, will guard your hearts and minds through Christ Jesus.
PHILIPPIANS 4:7 NKJV

REMEMBER THIS

Good thoughts can lead you to some very good places, and bad thoughts can lead elsewhere. So you must guard your thoughts accordingly.

A TIMELY TIP

If your inner voice is, in reality, your inner critic, you need to tone down the criticism now. And while you're at it, train yourself to begin thinking thoughts that are more rational, more accepting, and less judgmental.

9

WHEN YOU'RE DEALING WITH DIFFICULT TIMES, YOU MUST LEARN THE ART OF ACCEPTANCE

WHAT THE BIBLE SAYS

He is the LORD. He will do what He thinks is good.
1 SAMUEL 3:18 HCSB

If you're like most people, you like being in control. Period. You want things to happen according to your own wishes and according to your own timetable. But sometimes God has other plans, and He always has the final word.

Oswald Chambers correctly observed, "Our Lord never asks us to decide for Him; He asks us to yield to Him—a very different matter." These words remind us that even when we cannot understand the workings of God, we must trust Him and accept His will.

When Jesus went to the Mount of Olives, as described in Luke 22, He poured out His heart to the Lord. Jesus knew of the agony that He was destined to endure, but He also knew that God's will must be done. We, like our Savior, face trials that bring fear and trembling to the very depths of our souls, but like Christ, we too must ultimately seek God's will, not our own.

Are you embittered by a personal tragedy or a life-altering disappointment that you did not deserve and cannot fully understand? If so, it's time to make peace with life. It's time to forgive others and, if necessary, to forgive yourself. It's time to accept the unchangeable past, to embrace the priceless present, and to have faith in the promise of tomorrow. It's time to trust God completely. And it's time to reclaim the peace—His peace—that can and should be yours.

MORE THOUGHTS ABOUT THE ART OF ACCEPTANCE

Acceptance says, "True, this is my situation at the moment. I'll look unblinkingly at the reality of it. But, I'll also open my hands to accept willingly whatever a loving Father sends."

CATHERINE MARSHALL

The fruit of our placing all things in God's hands is the presence of His abiding peace in our hearts.

HANNAH WHITALL SMITH

One of the marks of spiritual maturity is the quiet confidence that God is in control, without the need to understand why He does what He does.

CHARLES SWINDOLL

Loving Him means the thankful acceptance of all things that His love has appointed.

ELISABETH ELLIOT

Accept each day as it comes to you. Do not waste your time and energy wishing for a different set of circumstances.

SARAH YOUNG

*Christians who are strong in the faith
grow as they accept whatever
God allows to enter their lives.*

BILLY GRAHAM

MORE FROM GOD'S WORD

*Should we accept only good things from
the hand of God and never anything bad?*

JOB 2:10 NLT

*Everything God made is good, and nothing
should be refused if it is accepted with thanks.*

1 TIMOTHY 4:4 NCV

*For now we see in a mirror, dimly,
but then face to face. Now I know in part,
but then I shall know just as I also am known.*

1 CORINTHIANS 13:12 NKJV

REMEMBER THIS

Once you accept the past—and make peace with it—you are free to live joyfully in the present. And that's precisely what you should do.

A TIMELY TIP

Acceptance means learning to trust God more. Today, think of at least one aspect of your life that you've been reluctant to accept, and then prayerfully ask God to help you trust Him more by accepting the past.

10
FAILURE ISN'T FINAL

WHAT THE BIBLE SAYS

One who listens to life-giving rebukes
will be at home among the wise.
Proverbs 15:31 HCSB

Life's occasional setbacks are simply the price that we must pay for our willingness to take risks as we follow our dreams. But even when we encounter bitter disappointments, we must never lose faith.

Hebrews 10:36 advises, "Patient endurance is what you need now, so that you will continue to do God's will. Then you will receive all that he has promised" (NLT). These words remind us that when we persevere, we will eventually receive the rewards that God has promised us. What's required is perseverance, not perfection.

When we face hardships, the Lord stands ready to protect us. Our responsibility, of course, is to ask Him for protection. When we call upon Him in heartfelt prayer, He will answer—in His own time and according to His own plan—and He will do His part to heal us. We, of course, must do our part too. And while we are waiting for God's plans to unfold and for His healing touch to restore us, we can be comforted in the knowledge that our Creator can overcome any obstacle, even if we cannot.

MORE THOUGHTS ABOUT FAILURE NOT BEING A PERMANENT CONDITION

*Never imagine that you can be
a loser by trusting in God.*

C. H. SPURGEON

*The enemy of our souls loves to taunt us
with past failures, wrongs, disappointments,
disasters, and calamities. And if we let him
continue doing this, our life becomes a long
and dark tunnel, with very little light at the end.*

CHARLES SWINDOLL

*Goals are worth setting and worth missing.
We learn from non-successes.*

BILL BRIGHT

*What may seem defeat to us
may be victory to Him.*

C. H. SPURGEON

*Often the doorway to success
is entered through the hallway of failure.*

ERWIN LUTZER

*If I succeed, I will give thanks.
If I fail, I will seek His grace.*

MAX LUCADO

MORE FROM GOD'S WORD

For though the righteous fall seven times,
they rise again.
PROVERBS 24:16 NIV

The LORD is near to those who
have a broken heart.
PSALM 34:18 NKJV

If you listen to correction to improve your life,
you will live among the wise.
PROVERBS 15:31 NCV

REMEMBER THIS

Almost every major failure in life—whether it's related to love, career, health, money, or anything else—is simply the result of many little failures along the way that were not attended to. Little failures add up if you let them. So don't let them.

A TIMELY TIP

Setbacks are inevitable, but your response to them is optional. You can always find a way to turn a stumbling block into a stepping stone. And you should.

11

THE LORD IS YOUR PROTECTOR IN GOOD TIMES AND DIFFICULT TIMES

WHAT THE BIBLE SAYS

The LORD is my shepherd, I shall not want.
He makes me lie down in green pastures; He leads
me beside quiet waters. He restores my soul.

PSALM 23:1–3 NASB

Time and again, the Bible promises that the Lord will protect those of us who honor and obey Him. But because we are imperfect human beings living imperfect lives, we worry. Even though we, as Christians, have the assurance of eternal life—even though we, as believers, have the promise of God's love and protection—we find ourselves fretting over the countless details of everyday life.

The Lord knows everything about His creation, and He keeps a watchful eye on His children. Whether we're in the heart of the big city, the far corner of the back forty, or anywhere in between, the Creator watches over us and protects us.

The Lord is our greatest refuge. When every earthly support system fails, He remains steadfast, and His love remains unchanged. When we encounter life's inevitable disappointments and setbacks, the Father remains faithful. When we suffer, He is always with us, always ready to respond to our prayers, always working in us and through us to turn tragedy into triumph.

Thankfully, even when there's nowhere else to turn, we can turn our thoughts and prayers to the Lord, and He will respond.

Even during life's most difficult days, God stands by us. Our job, of course, is to return the favor and stand by Him.

THE LORD IS SUFFICIENT TO MEET EVERY NEED

My grace is sufficient for you,
for my power is made perfect in weakness.
2 CORINTHIANS 12:9 NIV

Do the demands of life seem overwhelming at times? If so, you must learn to rely not only upon your own resources, but also upon the promises of your Father in heaven. God will hold your hand and walk with you and your family if you let Him. So even if your circumstances are difficult, trust the Father.

The psalmist writes, "Weeping may endure for a night, but joy comes in the morning" (Psalm 30:5 NKJV). But when we are suffering, the morning may seem very far away. It is not. God promises that He is "near to those who have a broken heart" (Psalm 34:18). When we are troubled, we must turn to Him, and we must encourage our friends and family members to do likewise.

If you are discouraged by the inevitable demands of life here on earth, be mindful of this fact: The loving heart of God is sufficient to meet any challenge, including yours. In good times and hard times, the Lord is always sufficient to meet your needs. No exceptions.

As Peter Marshall stated so well, "God is sufficient for all our needs, for every problem, for every difficulty, for every broken heart, for every human sorrow."

MORE THOUGHTS ABOUT
GOD'S PROTECTION

*Measure the size of the obstacles
against the size of God.*

BETH MOORE

*Only believe, don't fear. Our Master, Jesus, always
watches over us, and no matter what
the persecution, Jesus will surely overcome it.*

LOTTIE MOON

*The safest place in all the world is in
the will of God, and the safest protection
in all the world is the name of God.*

WARREN WIERSBE

*As you walk through the valley of the unknown,
you will find the footprints of Jesus both
in front of you and beside you.*

CHARLES STANLEY

*A mighty fortress is our God, a bulwark never failing,
our helper He amid the flood of mortal ills prevailing.*

MARTIN LUTHER

*The promises of God's Word sustain us in our
suffering, and we know Jesus sympathizes
and empathizes with us in our darkest hour.*

BILL BRIGHT

MORE FROM GOD'S WORD

The LORD is my light and my salvation—
whom should I fear? The LORD is the stronghold
of my life—of whom should I be afraid?
PSALM 27:1 HCSB

The LORD is my rock, my fortress, and my deliverer,
my God, my mountain where I seek refuge.
My shield, the horn of my salvation,
my stronghold, my refuge, and my Savior.
2 SAMUEL 22:2–3 HCSB

Those who trust in the LORD are like Mount Zion.
It cannot be shaken; it remains forever.
PSALM 125:1 HCSB

REMEMBER THIS

God has promised to protect you, and He's going to keep that promise. So if you're worried or afraid, pray about it.

A TIMELY TIP

Earthly security is an illusion. Your only real security comes from the loving heart of God. If you seek maximum protection, there's only one place you can receive it: from an infinite God.

12

WE MUST ASK GOD FOR THE THINGS WE NEED

WHAT THE BIBLE SAYS

Ask, and it will be given to you; seek, and you will find; knock, and it will be opened to you. For everyone who asks receives, and he who seeks finds, and to him who knocks it will be opened.

MATTHEW 7:7–8 NASB

Have you fervently asked God to restore your hope for tomorrow? Have you asked Him for guidance and strength? If so, then you're continually inviting your Creator to reveal Himself in a variety of ways. As a follower of Christ, you must do no less.

Jesus made it clear to His disciples: they should petition God to meet their needs. So should we. Genuine, heartfelt prayer produces powerful changes in us and in our world. When we lift our hearts to the Lord, we open ourselves to a never-ending source of divine wisdom and infinite love.

Do you have questions about your future that you simply can't answer? Do you have needs that you simply can't meet by yourself? Do you sincerely seek to know God's purpose for your life? If so, ask Him for direction, for protection, and for strength—and then keep asking Him every day that you live. Whatever your need, no matter how great or small, pray about it and never lose hope. God is not just near; He is here, and He's perfectly capable of answering your prayers. Now, it's up to you to ask.

MORE THOUGHTS ABOUT ASKING GOD FOR THE THINGS YOU NEED

*God will help us become the people
we are meant to be, if only we will ask Him.*

HANNAH WHITALL SMITH

*We get into trouble when we think we know what
to do and we stop asking God if we're doing it.*

STORMIE OMARTIAN

*By asking in Jesus' name, we're making
a request not only in His authority,
but also for His interests and His benefit.*

SHIRLEY DOBSON

*Often I have made a request of God with earnest
pleadings even backed up with Scripture,
only to have Him say "no" because He had
something better in store.*

RUTH BELL GRAHAM

*We honor God by asking for great things when
they are a part of His promise. We dishonor Him
and cheat ourselves when we ask for
molehills where He has promised mountains.*

VANCE HAVNER

*When you pray for something,
God gives you something to do.*

A. R. BERNARD

MORE FROM GOD'S WORD

Until now you have asked for nothing in My name.
Ask and you will receive,
so that your joy may be complete.
JOHN 16:24 HCSB

Do not be anxious about anything, but in
everything, by prayer and petition,
with thanksgiving, present your requests to God.
PHILIPPIANS 4:6 NIV

The effective prayer of a righteous
man can accomplish much.
JAMES 5:16 NASB

REMEMBER THIS

If you want more from life, ask more from God. If you're pursuing worthy goals, ask for God's help—and keep asking—until, in His own time and in His own way, He answers your prayers.

A TIMELY TIP

Today, think of a specific need that is weighing heavily on your heart. Then spend a few quiet moments asking God for His guidance and for His help.

13

THE LORD WILL
RENEW YOUR SPIRIT

WHAT THE BIBLE SAYS

*You are being renewed in the spirit
of your minds; you put on the new self,
the one created according to God's likeness
in righteousness and purity of the truth.*

EPHESIANS 4:23–24 HCSB

Even the most inspired Christians can, from time to time, find themselves running on empty. The demands of daily life can drain us of our strength and rob us of the joy that is rightfully ours in Christ. When we find ourselves tired, discouraged, or worse, there is a source from which we can draw the power needed to recharge our spiritual batteries. That source is God.

God intends that His children lead joyous lives filled with abundance and peace. But sometimes abundance and peace seem very far away. It is then that we must turn to God for renewal, and when we do, He will restore us.

Are you experiencing difficult times? Turn your heart toward God in prayer. Are you weak or worried? Take the time—or, more accurately, make the time—to delve deeply into God's Holy Word. Are you spiritually depleted? Call upon fellow believers to support you, and call upon Christ to renew your spirit and your life. When you do, you'll discover that the Creator of the universe stands always ready and always able to create a new sense of wonderment and joy in you.

MORE THOUGHTS ABOUT RENEWING YOUR SPIRIT

He is the God of wholeness and restoration.
STORMIE OMARTIAN

*Walking with God leads to receiving
His intimate counsel, and counseling
leads to deep restoration.*
JOHN ELDREDGE

*The same voice that brought Lazarus
out of the tomb raised us to newness of life.*
C. H. SPURGEON

*When we reach the end of our strength,
wisdom, and personal resources, we enter
into the beginning of His glorious provisions.*
PATSY CLAIRMONT

*Troubles we bear trustfully can bring us
a fresh vision of God and a new outlook on life,
an outlook of peace and hope.*
BILLY GRAHAM

*God never promises to remove us from our
struggles. He does promise, however,
to change the way we look at them.*
MAX LUCADO

MORE FROM GOD'S WORD

*Therefore, if anyone is in Christ, he is a new
creation; old things have passed away;
behold, all things have become new.*

2 CORINTHIANS 5:17 NKJV

*Those who hope in the LORD will renew their
strength. They will soar on wings like eagles;
they will run and not grow weary,
they will walk and not be faint.*

ISAIAH 40:31 NIV

*Finally, brothers, rejoice. Become mature,
be encouraged, be of the same mind,
be at peace, and the God of love
and peace will be with you.*

2 CORINTHIANS 13:11 HCSB

REMEMBER THIS

God can make all things new, including you. When you are weak or
worried, He can renew your spirit and restore your strength. Your
job, of course, is to let Him.

A TIMELY TIP

God wants to give you peace, and He wants to renew your spirit.
But He won't force you to experience the peace that passes all under-
standing. It's up to you to slow down, to study His Word, to ask for
His guidance, and to respond accordingly.

14

IN EVERY SEASON OF LIFE, GOD PROVIDES OPPORTUNITIES FOR RENEWAL AND GROWTH

WHAT THE BIBLE SAYS

Remember ye not the former things,
neither consider the things of old.
Behold, I will do a new thing.
ISAIAH 43:18–19 KJV

As you look at the landscape of your life, do you see opportunities, possibilities, and blessings, or do you focus, instead, upon the more negative scenery? Do you believe the Bible promise that God is making all things new—including you—or do you believe that's a promise that only applies to other people? If you've acquired the unfortunate habit of focusing too intently upon the negative aspects of your life, then your spiritual vision is in need of correction.

Whether you realize it or not, opportunities are whirling around you like stars crossing the night sky: beautiful to observe, but too numerous to count. Yet you may be too concerned with the challenges of everyday living to notice those opportunities. That's why you should slow down occasionally, catch your breath, and focus your thoughts on two things: the talents God has given you and the opportunities that He has placed before you. The Lord is leading you in the direction of those opportunities. Your task is to watch carefully, to pray fervently, and to be watchful for the opportunities He places along your path.

If you're consistently looking for the silver linings instead of the clouds, you'll discover that opportunities have a way of turning up in the most unexpected places. But if you've acquired the unfortunate habit of looking for problems instead of possibilities, you'll find that troubles have a way of turning up in unexpected places too. Since you're likely to find what you're looking for, why not look for opportunities? They're out there. And the rest is up to you.

MORE THOUGHTS ABOUT OPPORTUNITIES

Have thy tools ready; God will find thee work.
CHARLES KINGSLEY

Each day is God's gift of a fresh unspoiled opportunity to live according to His priorities.
ELIZABETH GEORGE

The past is our teacher; the present is our opportunity; the future is our friend.
EDWIN LOUIS COLE

A possibility is a hint from God.
SØREN KIERKEGAARD

We are all faced with a series of great opportunities brilliantly disguised as impossible situations.
CHARLES SWINDOLL

Alleged "impossibilities" are opportunities for our capacities to be stretched.
CHARLES SWINDOLL

MORE FROM GOD'S WORD

But as it is written:
What eye did not see and ear did not hear, and
what never entered the human mind—
God prepared this for those who love Him.
1 CORINTHIANS 2:9 HCSB

Whenever we have the opportunity,
we should do good to everyone—
especially to those in the family of faith.
GALATIANS 6:10 NLT

I can do all things through Christ
which strengtheneth me.
PHILIPPIANS 4:13 KJV

REMEMBER THIS

God constantly arrives at our doorsteps with countless opportunities. And He knocks. Our challenge, of course, is to open the door.

A TIMELY TIP

Every earthly opportunity has an expiration date. Your challenge is to discover the opportunities that God has placed before you—and to make the most of those opportunities—before they expire.

15

THE LORD WILL HELP YOU MEET ANY CHALLENGE

WHAT THE BIBLE SAYS

So we may boldly say: "The LORD is my helper; I will not fear. What can man do to me?"

HEBREWS 13:6 NKJV

Are you a confident believer, or do you live under a cloud of uncertainty and doubt? As a Christian, you have many reasons to be confident. After all, God is in His heaven; Christ has risen; and you are the recipient of God's grace. Despite these blessings, you may, from time to time, find yourself being tormented by negative emotions, and you are certainly not alone.

Even the most faithful Christians are overcome by occasional bouts of fear and doubt. You are no different. Every life—including yours—is a series of successes and failures, celebrations and disappointments, joys and sorrows, hopes and doubts.

Doubts come in several shapes and sizes: doubts about God, doubts about the future, and doubts about your own abilities, for starters. And what, precisely, does God's Word say in response to these doubts? The Bible is clear: when you are beset by doubts, of whatever kind, you must draw closer to God through worship and through prayer (James 4:8).

The Lord promises that He will never leave your side, not for an instant. He is always with you, always willing to calm the storms of life. When you sincerely seek His presence—and when you genuinely seek to establish a deeper, more meaningful relationship with

His Son—God is prepared to touch your heart, to calm your fears, to answer your doubts, and to restore your confidence.

MORE THOUGHTS ABOUT CONFIDENCE

*You cannot have a positive life
and a negative mind.*
JOYCE MEYER

Never yield to gloomy anticipation.
LETTIE COWMAN

*Confidence in the natural world is self-reliance;
in the spiritual world, it is God-reliance.*
OSWALD CHAMBERS

*We never get anywhere—nor do our
conditions and circumstances change—
when we look at the dark side of life.*
LETTIE COWMAN

*You need to make the right decision—
firmly and decisively—
and then stick with it, with God's help.*
BILLY GRAHAM

*Faith in God is the greatest power,
but great, too, is faith in oneself.*
MARY MCLEOD BETHUNE

MORE FROM GOD'S WORD

*Be strong and courageous,
and do the work. Don't be afraid
or discouraged, for the LORD God,
my God, is with you. He won't
leave you or forsake you.*
1 CHRONICLES 28:20 HCSB

*God is our refuge and strength,
a very present help in trouble.*
PSALM 46:1 NKJV

*You are my hope; O Lord GOD,
You are my confidence.*
PSALM 71:5 NASB

REMEMBER THIS

Confidence in yourself is fine, but what you need most of all is confidence in God.

A TIMELY TIP

As a Christian, you have every reason to be confident. With God as your partner, you have nothing to fear.

16

THE POWER OF ENTHUSIASM

WHAT THE BIBLE SAYS

*Whatever you do, do it enthusiastically, as
something done for the Lord and not for men.*
COLOSSIANS 3:23 HCSB

Are you enthusiastic about your life and your faith? Hopefully so.
But if, during difficult times, your zest for life has waned, it is now
time to redirect your efforts and recharge your spiritual batteries.
And that means refocusing your priorities (by putting God first)
and counting your blessings (instead of your problems).

Nothing is more important than your wholehearted commitment to your Creator and to His only begotten Son. Your faith must
never be an afterthought; it must be your ultimate priority, your
ultimate possession, and your ultimate passion. When you become
passionate about your faith, you'll become passionate about your
life too.

Genuine, heartfelt, enthusiastic Christianity is contagious. If
you enjoy a life-altering relationship with God, that relationship
will have an impact on others—perhaps a profound impact.

Are you constantly praising God for His gifts, and are you
sharing His Good News with the world? And are you excited about
the possibilities for service that the Lord has placed before you,
whether at home, at work, at church, or at school? You should be.
The world deserves your enthusiasm, and you deserve the experience of sharing it.

MORE THOUGHTS ABOUT ENTHUSIASM

It's easy to have a great attitude when things are going our way. It's when difficult challenges rise before us that attitude becomes the difference maker.

JOHN MAXWELL

It is a remarkable thing that some of the most optimistic and enthusiastic people you will meet are those who have been through intense suffering.

WARREN WIERSBE

Wherever you are, be all there. Live to the hilt every situation you believe to be the will of God.

JIM ELLIOT

Those who have achieved excellence in the practice of an art or profession have commonly been motivated by great enthusiasm in their pursuit of it.

JOHN KNOX

One of the great needs in the church today is for every Christian to become enthusiastic about his faith in Jesus Christ.

BILLY GRAHAM

We act as though comfort and luxury were the chief requirements of life, when all that we need to make us really happy is something to be enthusiastic about.

CHARLES KINGSLEY

MORE FROM GOD'S WORD

Do your work with enthusiasm.
Work as if you were serving the Lord,
not as if you were serving only men and women.
EPHESIANS 6:7 NCV

Rejoice always! Pray constantly.
Give thanks in everything,
for this is God's will for you in Christ Jesus.
1 THESSALONIANS 5:16–18 HCSB

Let the hearts of those who seek
the LORD rejoice. Look to the LORD
and his strength; seek his face always.
1 CHRONICLES 16:10–11 NIV

REMEMBER THIS

As a Christian, you have many reasons to be excited about your life, your future, and the promise of eternal life. Every day presents another opportunity to share your faith and your enthusiasm with a world that needs both.

A TIMELY TIP

Don't wait for enthusiasm to find you; make it your job to find it. Look at your life and your relationships as exciting adventures. Don't wait for life to spice itself; spice things up yourself.

17

YOU CAN LEARN TO
CONTROL YOUR EMOTIONS

WHAT THE BIBLE SAYS

*For this very reason, make every effort
to supplement your faith with goodness,
goodness with knowledge, knowledge
with self-control, self-control with endurance,
endurance with godliness.*

2 Peter 1:5–6 HCSB

Time and again, the Bible instructs us to live by faith. Yet despite our best intentions, negative feelings can rob us of the peace and abundance that could be ours—and should be ours—through Christ. When doubt, discouragement, frustration, impatience, or anxiety separates us from the spiritual blessings that God has in store, we must rethink our priorities. And we must place faith above feelings.

Human emotions are highly variable, decidedly unpredictable, and often unreliable. Our emotions are like the weather, only far more fickle. So we must learn to live by faith, not by the ups and downs of our own emotional roller coasters.

Sometime during this day, you will probably be gripped by a strong negative emotion. Distrust it. Rein it in. Test it. And turn it over to God. Your emotions will inevitably change; God will not. So trust Him completely as you watch your feelings slowly evaporate into thin air—which, of course, they will.

MORE THOUGHTS ABOUT
DEALING WITH EMOTIONS

*A life lived in God is not lived on the plane
of feelings, but of the will.*

ELISABETH ELLIOT

*I do not need to feel good or be ecstatic
in order to be in the center of God's will.*

BILL BRIGHT

*While walking through a dark season, if we attempt
to navigate our lives by what we feel, we will run
aground onto the rocks. We must navigate by
what we know is true no matter what we feel.*

SHEILA WALSH

*I may no longer depend on pleasant impulses
to bring me before the Lord. I must rather
respond to principles I know to be right,
whether I feel them to be enjoyable or not.*

JIM ELLIOT

*Don't bother much about your feelings. When they
are humble, loving, brave, give thanks for them;
when they are conceited, selfish, cowardly,
ask to have them altered. In neither case are
they you, but only a thing that happens to you.
What matters is your intentions and your behavior.*

C. S. LEWIS

MORE FROM GOD'S WORD

Grow a wise heart—you'll do yourself a favor;
keep a clear head—you'll find a good life.
PROVERBS 19:8 MSG

And let the peace of God rule in your hearts,
to which also you were called
in one body; and be thankful.
COLOSSIANS 3:15 NKJV

Enthusiasm without knowledge is not good.
If you act too quickly, you might make a mistake.
PROVERBS 19:2 NCV

REMEMBER THIS

The next time you encounter a difficult situation, be aware of your emotions. And don't allow other people's negative emotions to become your negative emotions.

A TIMELY TIP

Your life shouldn't be ruled by your emotions; your life should be ruled by God. So if you think you've lost control over your emotions, don't make big decisions, don't strike out against anybody, and don't speak out in anger. Count to ten (or more) and take "time out" from your situation until you can calm yourself down.

18
FEAR NOT

WHAT THE BIBLE SAYS

Fear not, for I am with you;
be not dismayed, for I am your God.
I will strengthen you, yes,
I will help you, I will uphold you
with My righteous right hand.
ISAIAH 41:10 NKJV

We live in a fear-based world, a world where bad news travels at light speed and good news doesn't. These are troubled times, times when we have legitimate fears for the future of our nation, our world, and our families. But as Christians, we have every reason to live courageously. After all, the ultimate battle has already been fought and won on that faraway cross at Calvary.

Perhaps you, like countless other believers, have found your courage tested by the anxieties and fears that are an inevitable part of twenty-first-century life. If so, God wants to have a little chat with you. The next time you find your courage tested to the limit, the Lord wants to remind you that He is not just near; He is here.

Your heavenly Father is your Protector and your Deliverer. Call upon Him in your hour of need, and be comforted. Whatever your challenge, whatever your trouble, God can handle it. And will.

MORE THOUGHTS ABOUT FEAR

*Seeing that a pilot steers the ship in which
we sail, who will never allow us to perish
even in the midst of shipwrecks, there is
no reason why our minds should be overwhelmed
with fear and overcome with weariness.*

JOHN CALVIN

*It is good to remind ourselves that
the will of God comes from the heart of God
and that we need not be afraid.*

WARREN WIERSBE

*The Lord Jesus by His Holy Spirit is with me,
and the knowledge of His presence dispels
the darkness and allays any fears.*

BILL BRIGHT

*You needn't worry about not feeling brave.
Our Lord didn't—see the scene in Gethsemane.
How thankful I am that when God became man
He did not choose to become a man of
iron nerves; that would not have helped
weaklings like you and me nearly so much.*

C. S. LEWIS

*The presence of fear does not mean you have
no faith. Fear visits everyone. But make your
fear a visitor and not a resident.*

MAX LUCADO

MORE FROM GOD'S WORD

Peace I leave with you; My peace
I give to you; not as the world gives do
I give to you. Do not let your heart
be troubled, nor let it be fearful.
JOHN 14:27 NASB

The LORD is my light and my salvation—
whom should I fear? The LORD is the
stronghold of my life—of whom should I be afraid?
PSALM 27:1 HCSB

Even though I walk through the darkest valley,
I will fear no evil, for you are with me;
your rod and your staff, they comfort me.
PSALM 23:4 NIV

REMEMBER THIS

You must trust God to handle the problems that are simply too big for you to solve. Because the Lord is your shepherd, you can entrust the future—your future—to Him.

A TIMELY TIP

Everybody faces obstacles. Don't overestimate the size of yours. And instead of fretting about your setbacks, ask the Lord to help you find the courage and the strength to pick yourself up and try again.

AVOID NEEDLESS AND FRUITLESS COMPLAINTS

WHAT THE BIBLE SAYS

Be hospitable to one another without complaining.
1 PETER 4:9 HCSB

Most of us have more blessings than we can count, yet we can still find reasons to complain about the minor frustrations of everyday life. To do so, of course, is not only shortsighted, but it is also a serious roadblock on the path to spiritual abundance.

Would you like to feel more comfortable about your circumstances and your life? Then promise yourself that you'll do whatever it takes to focus your thoughts and energy on the major blessings you've received, not the minor inconveniences you must occasionally endure.

So the next time you're tempted to complain about the inevitable frustrations of everyday living, resist that temptation. Instead, make it a practice to count your blessings, not your hardships. It's the truly decent way to live.

MORE THOUGHTS ABOUT BECOMING A COMPLAINT-FREE ZONE

If we have our eyes upon ourselves, our problems, and our pain, we cannot lift our eyes upward.
BILLY GRAHAM

*It is always possible to be thankful for
what is given rather than to complain
about what is not given. One or
the other becomes a habit of life.*

ELISABETH ELLIOT

*Don't complain. The more you complain
about things, the more things
you'll have to complain about.*

E. STANLEY JONES

*Grumbling and gratitude are, for the child of God,
in conflict. Be grateful and you won't grumble.
Grumble and you won't be grateful.*

BILLY GRAHAM

*Thanksgiving or complaining—these words
express two contrasting attitudes of the souls
of God's children. The soul that gives thanks
can find comfort in everything; the soul
that complains can find comfort in nothing.*

HANNAH WHITALL SMITH

*Whenever anything disagreeable
or displeasing happens to you,
remember Christ crucified and be silent.*

ST. JOHN OF THE CROSS

MORE FROM GOD'S WORD

Do everything without complaining or arguing.
Then you will be innocent and without any wrong.
PHILIPPIANS 2:14–15 NCV

Those who guard their lips preserve their lives,
but those who speak rashly will come to ruin.
PROVERBS 13:3 NIV

My dear brothers and sisters, always be
willing to listen and slow to speak.
JAMES 1:19 NCV

REMEMBER THIS

Constant complaints are roadblocks on the path to success. You'll never complain your way to the top, so don't even try.

A TIMELY TIP

If you feel a personal pity party coming on, slow down and start counting your blessings. If you fill your heart with gratitude, there's simply no room left for complaints.

20

GOD'S FORGIVENESS IS ALWAYS AVAILABLE

WHAT THE BIBLE SAYS

*If we confess our sins, He is faithful
and righteous to forgive us our sins and
to cleanse us from all unrighteousness.*

1 JOHN 1:9 NASB

All of us have sinned. Sometimes our sins result from our own stubborn rebellion against God's commandments. Sometimes we are swept up by events that encourage us to behave in ways that we later come to regret. And sometimes, even when our intentions are honorable, we make mistakes that have long-lasting consequences. When we look back at our actions with remorse, we may experience intense feelings of guilt, but God has an answer for the guilt that we feel. That answer, of course, is His forgiveness.

Are you troubled by feelings of guilt, even after you've received the Lord's forgiveness? Are you still struggling with painful memories of mistakes you made long ago? Are you focused so intently on yesterday that your vision of today is clouded? If so, you still have work to do—spiritual work.

Once you have asked God for His forgiveness, you can be certain that your heavenly Father has given it. And if He, in His infinite wisdom, has forgiven your sins, how then can you withhold forgiveness from yourself? The answer, of course, is that once God has forgiven you, you should forgive yourself too.

When you forgive yourself thoroughly and completely, you'll

stop investing energy in those most useless of emotions: bitterness, regret, guilt, and self-recrimination. And you can then get busy making the world a better place, and that's as it should be. After all, since God has forgiven you, isn't it about time that you demonstrate your gratitude by serving Him?

MORE THOUGHTS ABOUT GOD'S FORGIVENESS

*God's mercy is boundless, free,
and, through Jesus Christ our Lord,
available to us in our present situation.*

A. W. TOZIER

*Forgiveness is an opportunity that God
extended to us on the cross. When we
accept His forgiveness and are willing
to forgive ourselves, then we find relief.*

BILLY GRAHAM

We cannot out-sin God's ability to forgive us.

BETH MOORE

*The most marvelous ingredient in the forgiveness
of God is that He also forgets, the one thing
a human being cannot do. With God, forgetting
is a divine attribute. God's forgiveness forgets.*

OSWALD CHAMBERS

*God does not wish us to remember
what He is willing to forget.*

GEORGE A. BUTTRICK

MORE FROM GOD'S WORD

*All the prophets testify about Him that
through His name everyone who believes
in Him will receive forgiveness of sins.*
Acts 10:43 HCSB

*Let us, then, feel very sure that we can
come before God's throne where there
is grace. There we can receive mercy
and grace to help us when we need it.*
Hebrews 4:16 NCV

*But the mercy of the Lord is from everlasting
to everlasting upon them that fear him,
and his righteousness unto children's children.*
Psalm 103:17 KJV

REMEMBER THIS

If you've asked for God's forgiveness, He has given it. But have you forgiven yourself? If not, the best moment to do so is this one.

A TIMELY TIP

You cannot do anything that God can't forgive. The Lord stands ready, willing, and able to forgive you, no matter your circumstances, no matter your past. And the next move is yours.

21

GOD HAS GIVEN YOU TALENTS, AND HE WANTS YOU TO USE THEM

WHAT THE BIBLE SAYS

*I remind you to keep ablaze
the gift of God that is in you.*
2 TIMOTHY 1:6 HCSB

All of us have special talents, and you are no exception. But your talent is no guarantee of success; it must be cultivated and nurtured; otherwise, it will go unused, and God's gift to you will be squandered.

In Matthew 25, Jesus tells the parable of the talents. In it, He describes a master who leaves his servants with varying amounts of money (talents). When the master returns, some servants have put their money to work and earned more, to which the master responds, "Well done, good and faithful servant! You have been faithful with a few things; I will put you in charge of many things. Come and share your master's happiness!" (Matthew 25:21 NIV).

But the story does not end so happily for the foolish servant who was given a single talent but did nothing with it. For this man, the master has nothing but reproach: "You wicked, lazy servant!" (Matthew 25:26). The message from Jesus is clear: we must use our talents, not waste them.

Your particular talent is a treasure on temporary loan from the Creator. He intends that your talent enrich the world and enrich your life. Even when you're enduring difficult times, you must value the gift that the Lord has given you. And you must share your talents with the world. Then when you meet your Master face-to-face, you, too, will hear those wonderful words, "Well done, good and faithful servant! . . . Come and share your Master's happiness!"

MORE THOUGHTS ABOUT USING YOUR TALENTS

If others don't use their gifts, you get cheated, and if you don't use your gifts, they get cheated.
RICK WARREN

You are the only person on earth who can use your ability.
ZIG ZIGLAR

Employ whatever God has entrusted you with, in doing good, all possible good, in every possible kind and degree.
JOHN WESLEY

If you want to reach your potential, you need to add a strong work ethic to your talent.
JOHN MAXWELL

You aren't an accident. You were deliberately planned, specifically gifted, and lovingly positioned on this earth by the Master Craftsman.
MAX LUCADO

It is true that we may desire much more. But let us use what we have, and God will give us more.

ADONIRAM JUDSON

MORE FROM GOD'S WORD

Do not neglect the gift that is in you.
1 TIMOTHY 4:14 NKJV

God has given each of you a gift from his great variety of spiritual gifts. Use them well to serve one another.
1 PETER 4:10 NLT

Now there are diversities of gifts, but the same Spirit.
1 CORINTHIANS 12:4 KJV

REMEMBER THIS

Converting raw talent into polished skill usually requires work, and lots of it. And God's Word clearly instructs you to do the hard work of refining your talents for the glory of His kingdom and the service of His people.

A TIMELY TIP

You are wise to remember this old adage: "What you are is God's gift to you; what you become is your gift to God." And it's up to you to make sure that your gift is worthy of the Giver.

22

IT'S IMPORTANT TO GET ENOUGH REST

WHAT THE BIBLE SAYS

*Come unto me, all ye that labor
and are heavy laden, and I will give you rest.*
Matthew 11:28 KJV

Tough times can sow seeds of doubt and fear. To combat those negative emotions, you need to be at your best, and to feel your best, you need to get enough sleep. But you inhabit an interconnected world that never slows down and never shuts off. The world tempts you to stay up late watching the news or surfing the Internet or checking out social media or gaming, or doing countless other activities that gobble up your time and distract you from more important tasks. But too much late-night screen time robs you of the sleep you need to meet the challenges of everyday life.

Are you going to bed at a reasonable hour and sleeping through the night? If so, you're both wise and blessed. But if you're staying up late with your eyes glued to a screen, you're putting your long-term health at risk. And you're probably wasting time too.

So the next time you're tempted to engage in late-night, time-wasting activities, resist the temptation. Instead, turn your thoughts and prayers to God. And when you're finished, turn off the lights and go to bed. You need rest more than you need entertainment.

MORE THOUGHTS ABOUT REST

Jesus is calling the weary to rest,
Calling today, calling today,
Bring Him your burden and you shall be blest;
He will not turn you away.

FANNY CROSBY

He who cannot rest, cannot work;
he who cannot let go, cannot hold on;
he who cannot find footing, cannot go forward.

HARRY EMERSON FOSDICK

Life is strenuous. See that your
clock does not run down.

LETTIE COWMAN

Sweet shall be your rest if your
heart does not reproach you.

THOMAS À KEMPIS

Our Lord never drew power from Himself;
He drew it always from His Father.

OSWALD CHAMBERS

God specializes in giving people a fresh start.

RICK WARREN

MORE FROM GOD'S WORD

Those who hope in the Lord will renew their strength.
They will soar on wings like eagles; they will run and
not grow weary, they will walk and not be faint.
Isaiah 40:31 NIV

Finally, brothers, rejoice. Become mature,
be encouraged, be of the same mind,
be at peace, and the God of love
and peace will be with you.
2 Corinthians 13:11 HCSB

Now the God of all grace, who called
you to His eternal glory in Christ Jesus,
will personally restore, establish,
strengthen, and support you.
1 Peter 5:10 HCSB

REMEMBER THIS

It takes energy to do your work and to do God's work. If you want to be an effective servant, you should be a well-rested servant.

A TIMELY TIP

If your fuse is chronically short, or if you're always tired, perhaps you need a little more sleep. Try this experiment: Turn off all screens and go to bed at a reasonable hour. You'll be amazed at how good you feel when you get eight hours of sleep.

23

CORRECT YOUR MISTAKES AND MOVE ON

WHAT THE BIBLE SAYS

He who covers his sins will not prosper,
but whoever confesses
and forsakes them will have mercy.

PROVERBS 28:13 NKJV

Everybody makes mistakes, and so will you. In fact, Winston Churchill once observed, "Success is going from failure to failure without loss of enthusiasm." What was good for Churchill is also good for you. You should expect to make mistakes—plenty of them—but you should not allow those missteps to rob you of the enthusiasm you need to fulfill God's plan for your life.

We are imperfect people living in an imperfect world; mistakes are simply part of the price we pay for being here. But even though mistakes are an inevitable part of life's journey, *repeated* mistakes should not be. When we commit the inevitable blunders of life, we must correct them, learn from them, and pray for the wisdom not to repeat them. When we do, our mistakes become lessons, and our experiences become adventures in character building.

Have you made a king-size blunder or two? Of course you have. But here's the big question: Have you used your mistakes as stumbling blocks or stepping stones? The answer to this question will determine the quality of your day and the direction of your life. So don't let the fear of past failures hold you back. Instead, own up to your mistakes, do your best to fix them, and be sure to learn from them. And while you're at it, please remember this: even if you've made a colossal blunder, God isn't finished with you yet—in fact, He's probably just getting started.

MORE THOUGHTS ABOUT LEARNING FROM MISTAKES

*Father, take our mistakes
and turn them into opportunities.*
MAX LUCADO

*Truth will sooner come out
of error than from confusion.*
FRANCIS BACON

*Lord, when we are wrong, make us
willing to change; and when we are right,
make us easy to live with.*
PETER MARSHALL

*Very few things motivate us to give God our
undivided attention like being faced with
the negative consequences of our decisions.*
CHARLES STANLEY

*I hope you don't mind me telling you all this.
One can learn only by seeing one's mistakes.*
C. S. LEWIS

*One mistake does not have
to rule a person's entire life.*
JOYCE MEYER

MORE FROM GOD'S WORD

Therefore let us approach the throne
of grace with boldness, so that
we may receive mercy and find grace
to help us at the proper time.
HEBREWS 4:16 HCSB

Be merciful, just as your Father is merciful.
LUKE 6:36 NIV

Therefore, if anyone is in Christ, he is a new
creation; old things have passed away;
behold, all things have become new.
2 CORINTHIANS 5:17 NKJV

REMEMBER THIS

Everybody makes mistakes, and you will make them too. So don't let occasional mistakes dominate your life. It's better to focus on repairing your mistakes than fretting about them.

A TIMELY TIP

When you make a mistake, the time to make things better is now, not later. The sooner you address your problem, the sooner you will make amends and move on.

24

BE OPTIMISTIC

WHAT THE BIBLE SAYS

The LORD is my light and my salvation—
whom should I fear?
The LORD is the stronghold of my life—
of whom should I be afraid?

PSALM 27:1 HCSB

Are you a passionate Christian who expects God to do big things in your life and in the lives of those around you? If you're a thinking Christian, you have every reason to be confident about your future here on earth and your eternal future in heaven. As English clergyman William Ralph Inge observed, "No Christian should be a pessimist, for Christianity is a system of radical optimism." Inge's observation is true, of course, but sometimes, you may find yourself caught up in the inevitable complications that accompany tough times. When you find yourself fretting about the inevitable ups and downs of life here on earth, it's time to slow down, refocus your thoughts, size up your opportunities, and count your blessings.

God has made promises to you, and He will most certainly keep every one of them. So you have every reason to be an optimist and no legitimate reason to ever abandon hope.

So today and every day, trust your hopes, not your fears. And while you're at it, take time to celebrate God's blessings. His gifts are too numerous to calculate and too glorious to imagine. But it never hurts to try.

YOUR VERY BRIGHT FUTURE

*There is surely a future hope for you,
and your hope will not be cut off.*

PROVERBS 23:18 NIV

If you've entrusted your heart to Christ, your eternal fate is secure and your future is eternally bright. No matter how troublesome your present circumstances may seem, you need not fear because the Lord has promised that you are His now and forever.

Of course, you won't be exempt from the normal challenges of life here on earth. While you're here, you'll probably experience your fair share of disappointments, emergencies, setbacks, and outright failures. But these are only temporary defeats.

Are you willing to place your future in the hands of a loving and all-knowing God? Do you trust in the ultimate goodness of His plan for you? Will you face today's challenges with hope and optimism? You should. After all, God created you for a very important purpose—His purpose. And you still have important work to do—His work. So today, as you live in the present and look to the future, remember that God has a marvelous plan for you. Act—and believe—accordingly.

Corrie ten Boom observed, "Every experience God gives us, every person He brings into our lives, is the perfect preparation for the future that only He can see."

MORE THOUGHTS ABOUT OPTIMISM

*Never yield to gloomy anticipation. Place your hope
and confidence in God. He has no record of failure.*

LETTIE COWMAN

Feed your mind with the good, the clean,
the pure, the powerful, and the positive.

ZIG ZIGLAR

The tough-minded optimist views any
problem as a challenge to his intelligence,
ingenuity, and faith. He keeps thinking,
praying, and believing. He knows there is
a solution, and he's determined to find it.

NORMAN VINCENT PEALE

All things work together for good.
Fret not, nor fear!

LETTIE COWMAN

Developing a positive attitude means
working continually to find what
is uplifting and encouraging.

BARBARA JOHNSON

Two types of voices command your
attention today. Negative ones fill your
mind with doubt, bitterness, and fear.
Positive ones purvey hope and strength.
Which one will you choose to heed?

MAX LUCADO

MORE FROM GOD'S WORD

Make me to hear joy and gladness.
Psalm 51:8 KJV

*But if we look forward to something we don't yet
have, we must wait patiently and confidently.*
Romans 8:25 NLT

*This hope we have as an anchor of the soul,
a hope both sure and steadfast.*
Hebrews 6:19 NASB

REMEMBER THIS

Optimism pays. Pessimism does not. Guard your thoughts and your words accordingly. This day, like every other day, is a good time to count your blessings and to think optimistically about your future.

A TIMELY TIP

Be a realistic optimist. Your attitude toward the future will help create your future. So think realistically about yourself and your situation while making a conscious effort to focus on hopes, not fears. When you do, you'll put the self-fulfilling prophecy to work for you.

25

WHEN IT NEEDS TO BE DONE, DO IT NOW

WHAT THE BIBLE SAYS

For the kingdom of God is not a matter of talk but of power.

1 CORINTHIANS 4:20 HCSB

When something needs to be done, the best time to do it is now, not later. But we're tempted to do otherwise. When the task at hand is difficult or unpleasant, we're tempted to procrastinate. But procrastination is the enemy of progress and a stumbling block on the path to success.

Are you in the habit of doing what needs to be done when it needs to be done? If you've acquired the habit of doing things sooner rather than later, congratulations! But if you find yourself putting off all those unpleasant tasks until later (or never), it's time to think about the consequences of your behavior.

One way that you can learn to defeat procrastination is by paying less attention to your fears and more attention to your responsibilities. So when you're faced with a difficult choice or an unpleasant responsibility, don't spend endless hours fretting over your fate. Simply seek God's counsel and get busy. When you do, you will be richly rewarded because of your willingness to act.

MORE THOUGHTS ABOUT TAKING ACTION NOW

Do noble things, do not dream them all day long.

CHARLES KINGSLEY

*Character is formed by doing the thing
we are supposed to do, when it should be done,
whether we feel like doing it or not.*

FATHER FLANAGAN

*Every difficult task that comes across your path—
every one that you would rather not do,
that will take the most effort, cause the most pain,
and be the greatest struggle—
brings a blessing with it.*

LETTIE COWMAN

*If doing a good act in public will excite others
to do more good, then "Let your Light shine to all."
Miss no opportunity to do good.*

JOHN WESLEY

*Now is the only time worth having because,
indeed, it is the only time we have.*

C. H. SPURGEON

*Every time you refuse to face up to life and its
problems, you weaken your character.*

E. STANLEY JONES

MORE FROM GOD'S WORD

Therefore, with your minds ready for action,
be serious and set your hope completely
on the grace to be brought to you at the
revelation of Jesus Christ.
1 PETER 1:13 HCSB

When you make a vow to God,
do not delay to fulfill it. He has no
pleasure in fools; fulfill your vow.
ECCLESIASTES 5:4 NIV

But prove yourselves doers of the word, and not
merely hearers who delude themselves.
JAMES 1:22 NASB

REMEMBER THIS

Because your actions always speak louder than your words, it's always the right time to let your actions speak for themselves.

A TIMELY TIP

Today, pick out one important obligation that you've been putting off. Then take at least one specific step toward the completion of the task you've been avoiding. Even if you don't finish the job, you'll discover that it's easier to finish a job that you've already begun than to finish a job that you've never started.

26

BEYOND ANGER

WHAT THE BIBLE SAYS

*Everyone must be quick to hear, slow to speak,
and slow to anger, for man's anger does not
accomplish God's righteousness.*

JAMES 1:19–20 HCSB

Anger is harmful, hurtful, and dangerous to your spiritual health because whenever your thoughts are hijacked by angry emotions, you inevitably forfeit the peace and perspective that might otherwise be yours. And to make matters worse, angry thoughts can cause you to behave in irrational, self-destructive ways. As the old saying goes, "Anger is only one letter away from danger."

When we've been hurt badly, we don't forget easily. When we can identify the person who hurt us, we naturally focus our ire on the perpetrator. Unless we can find the inner strength to forgive that person, we're likely to internalize the anger for years, for decades, or for a lifetime. Anger turned inward is always detrimental to our spiritual health and disruptive to our lives. And that's one reason—but not the only reason—that we should learn how to forgive other people quickly and completely. To do otherwise will result in needless anger and inner turmoil.

First Peter 5:8–9 warns, "Stay alert! Watch out for your great enemy, the devil. He prowls around like a roaring lion, looking for someone to devour. Stand firm against him, and be strong in your faith" (NLT). And of this you can be sure: Your adversary will use an unforgiving heart, and the inevitable anger that dwells within it, to sabotage your life and undermine your faith. To be safe, you must cleanse your heart, and you must forgive. You must say yes to God, yes to mercy, yes to love, and no to anger.

MORE THOUGHTS ABOUT ANGER

Anger breeds remorse in the heart,
discord in the home, bitterness in the community,
and confusion in the state.

BILLY GRAHAM

Bitterness and anger, usually over trivial things,
make havoc of homes, churches, and friendships.

WARREN WIERSBE

We must meet our disappointments,
our malicious enemies, our provoking friends,
our trials of every sort, with an attitude
of surrender and trust. We must rise above them
in Christ so they lose their power to harm us.

HANNAH WHITALL SMITH

Anger is the noise of the soul; the unseen irritant
of the heart; the relentless invader of silence.

MAX LUCADO

It takes strength to acknowledge our anger,
and sometimes more strength yet to curb
the aggressive urges anger may bring and
to channel them into nonviolent outlets.

FRED ROGERS

MORE FROM GOD'S WORD

*But I tell you that anyone who is angry with a
brother or sister will be subject to judgment.*
MATTHEW 5:22 NIV

*He who is slow to wrath has great understanding,
but he who is impulsive exalts folly.*
PROVERBS 14:29 NKJV

*A hot-tempered man stirs up conflict,
but a man slow to anger calms strife.*
PROVERBS 15:18 HCSB

REMEMBER THIS

Angry outbursts can be dangerous to your emotional and spiritual health, not to mention your relationships. So treat anger as an uninvited guest, and usher it away as quickly—and as quietly—as possible.

A TIMELY TIP

If you're tempted to explode in anger, resist the temptation. Instead of responding angrily, it's usually better to slow down, catch your breath, consider your options, and walk away if you must. Striking out in anger can lead to big problems, so it's better to walk away—and keep walking—than to blurt out angry words that can't be un-blurted.

27

WHEN YOU'RE DEALING WITH DIFFICULT TIMES, THE LORD WILL SUSTAIN YOU

WHAT THE BIBLE SAYS

*Cast your burden on the LORD,
and He shall sustain you;
He shall never permit the righteous to be moved.*
PSALM 55:22 NKJV

Because you have the ability to think, you also have the ability to worry. Even if you're a very faithful Christian, you may be plagued by occasional periods of discouragement and doubt. Even though you trust God's promise of eternal life—even though you sincerely believe in God's love and protection—you may find yourself upset by unfortunate circumstances that threaten to derail your plans or disrupt your life. Jesus understood your concerns when He spoke these reassuring words found in Matthew 6:

> Therefore I say to you, do not worry about your life, what you will eat or what you will drink; nor about your body, what you will put on. Is not life more than food and the body more than clothing? Look at the birds of the air, for they neither sow nor reap nor gather into barns; yet your heavenly Father feeds them. Are you not of more value than they? Which of you by worrying can add one cubit to his stature? . . . Therefore do not worry about tomorrow, for tomor-

row will worry about its own things. Sufficient for the day is its own trouble (vv. 25–27, 34 NKJV).

Where is the best place to take your worries? Take them to God. Take your troubles to Him; take your fears to Him; take your doubts to Him; take your weaknesses to Him; take your sorrows to Him, and leave them all there. Seek protection from the One who offers you eternal salvation; build your spiritual house upon the Rock that cannot be moved.

MORE THOUGHTS ABOUT OVERCOMING WORRY

Say to yourself, "Worry is just a very bad mental habit. And I can change any habit with God's help."
NORMAN VINCENT PEALE

The more you meditate on God's Word, the less you will have to worry about.
RICK WARREN

The beginning of anxiety is the end of faith, and the beginning of true faith is the end of anxiety.
GEORGE MUELLER

Much that worries us beforehand can, quite unexpectedly, have a happy and simple solution. Worries just don't matter. Things really are in a better hand than ours.
DIETRICH BONHOEFFER

*Every tomorrow has two handles: We can take
hold of the handle of anxiety or the handle of faith.*

HENRY WARD BEECHER

MORE FROM GOD'S WORD

*Do not be anxious about anything, but in
everything, by prayer and petition, with
thanksgiving, present your requests to God.*

PHILIPPIANS 4:6 NIV

*Let not your heart be troubled;
you believe in God, believe also in Me.*

JOHN 14:1 NKJV

*Cast all your anxiety on him
because he cares for you.*

1 PETER 5:7 NIV

REMEMBER THIS

You have worries, but God has solutions. Your challenge is to trust
Him to solve the problems that are simply too big for you to resolve
on your own.

A TIMELY TIP

Assiduously divide your areas of concern into two categories: those
you can control and those you cannot. Resolve never to waste time
or energy worrying about the latter.

28

PERSEVERANCE PAYS

WHAT THE BIBLE SAYS

For you have need of endurance,
so that when you have done the will of God,
you may receive what was promised.

HEBREWS 10:36 NASB

The next time you find your courage tested to the limit, remember that it pays to persevere. And remember that life's greatest victories are usually reserved for determined people (like you) who simply refuse to give up.

Occasionally, good things happen with little or no effort. Somebody wins the lottery or inherits a fortune or stumbles onto a financial bonanza by being at the right place at the right time. But more often than not, good things happen to people who work hard, and keep working hard, when just about everybody else has gone home or given up.

Every marathon has a finish line, and so does yours. So keep putting one foot in front of the other, pray for strength, and don't give up. Whether you realize it or not, you're up to the challenge if you persevere. And with God's help, that's exactly what you'll do.

Perhaps you are in a hurry for God to help you resolve your difficulties. Perhaps you're anxious to earn the rewards that you feel you've already earned from life. Perhaps you're drumming your fingers, impatiently waiting for God to act. If so, be forewarned: God operates on His own timetable, not yours. Sometimes the Lord may answer your prayers with silence, and when He does, you must patiently persevere. In times of trouble, you must remain steadfast and trust in the merciful goodness of your heavenly Father. Whatever your problem, He can manage it. Your job is to keep persevering until He does.

MORE THOUGHTS ABOUT PERSEVERANCE

Perseverance is more than endurance. It is endurance combined with absolute assurance and certainty that what we are looking for is going to happen.

OSWALD CHAMBERS

Don't quit. For if you do, you may miss the answer to your prayers.

MAX LUCADO

Press on. Obstacles are seldom the same size tomorrow as they are today.

ROBERT SCHULLER

Battles are won in the trenches, in the grit and grime of courageous determination; they are won day by day in the arena of life.

CHARLES SWINDOLL

Let us not cease to do the utmost, that we may incessantly go forward in the way of the Lord; and let us not despair of the smallness of our accomplishments.

JOHN CALVIN

MORE FROM GOD'S WORD

Let us not become weary in doing good,
for at the proper time we will reap
a harvest if we do not give up.
GALATIANS 6:9 NIV

But as for you, be strong; don't
be discouraged, for your work has a reward.
2 CHRONICLES 15:7 HCSB

So let us run the race that is before us
and never give up. We should remove from
our lives anything that would get in the way
and the sin that so easily holds us back.
HEBREWS 12:1 NCV

REMEMBER THIS

When things go wrong, it's easy to become discouraged. But a far better strategy is simply this: work hard to change the things you can change, and pray about the things you can't change.

A TIMELY TIP

Whenever you are being tested, you can call upon God, and you should. The Lord will give you the strength to persevere, and that's exactly what you should ask Him to do.

29

IN EVERY SEASON OF LIFE, KEEP GROWING

WHAT THE BIBLE SAYS

*I remind you to fan into flames
the spiritual gift God gave you.*

2 TIMOTHY 1:6 NLT

When it comes to your faith, God doesn't intend for you to stand still. He wants you to keep moving and growing. In fact, God's plan for you includes a lifetime of prayer, praise, and spiritual growth. When we cease to grow, either emotionally or spiritually, we do ourselves and our loved ones a profound disservice. But if we study God's Word, if we obey His commandments, and if we live in the center of His will, our faith will grow.

Many of life's most important lessons are painful to learn. During difficult times, we must be courageous and we must be patient, knowing that in His own time, the Lord will heal us if we invite Him into our hearts.

Spiritual growth need not take place only in times of adversity. We must seek to grow in our knowledge and love of the Lord every day that we live. In those quiet moments when we open our hearts to God, the One who made us keeps remaking us. He offers us guidance, perspective, wisdom, and courage. The appropriate moment to accept those spiritual gifts is the present one.

Are you as mature as you're ever going to be? Hopefully not! When it comes to your faith, God doesn't intend for you to become "fully grown," at least not in this lifetime. In fact, the Lord still has important lessons that He intends to teach you. So ask yourself this: What lesson is God trying to teach me today? And then go about the business of learning it.

MORE THOUGHTS ABOUT SPIRITUAL GROWTH

The vigor of our spiritual lives will be in exact proportion to the place held by the Bible in our lives and in our thoughts.
GEORGE MUELLER

Daily Bible reading is essential to victorious living and real Christian growth.
BILLY GRAHAM

The Scriptures were not given for our information, but for our transformation.
D. L. MOODY

Kindness in this world will do much to help others, not only to come into the light, but also to grow in grace day by day.
FANNY CROSBY

Grow, dear friends, but grow, I beseech you, in God's way, which is the only true way.
HANNAH WHITALL SMITH

MORE FROM GOD'S WORD

But grow in the grace and knowledge
of our Lord and Savior Jesus Christ. To Him
be the glory both now and forever. Amen.
2 PETER 3:18 NKJV

And be not conformed to this world: but be ye
transformed by the renewing of your mind,
that ye may prove what is that good, and
acceptable, and perfect will of God.
ROMANS 12:2 KJV

But endurance must do its complete work,
so that you may be mature
and complete, lacking nothing.
JAMES 1:4 HCSB

REMEMBER THIS

When it comes to your faith, the Lord doesn't want you to stand still. He wants you to keep growing. Your intentions should be the same.

A TIMELY TIP

Times of change can be times of growth. So remember: spiritual maturity is always a journey, never a destination.

30
THE POWER OF PRAYER
WHAT THE BIBLE SAYS

*The earnest prayer of a righteous person has
great power and produces wonderful results.*
James 5:16 NLT

Does prayer play an important role in your life? Is prayer an integral part of your daily routine or is it a hit-or-miss activity? Do you "pray without ceasing," or is your prayer life an afterthought? If you genuinely wish to receive that abundance that Christ promises in John 10:10, then you must pray constantly. And you must never underestimate the power of prayer.

As you contemplate the quality of your prayer life, here are a few things to consider:

1. God hears our prayers and answers them (Jeremiah 29:11–12).
2. God promises that the prayers of righteous men and women can accomplish great things (James 5:16).
3. God invites us to be still and to feel His presence (Psalm 46:10).

So pray. Start praying in the early morning and keep praying until you fall off to sleep at night. Pray about matters great and small; and be watchful for the answers that God most assuredly sends your way.

Daily prayer and meditation is a matter of will and habit. When you organize your day to include quiet moments with the Lord, you'll soon discover that no time is more precious than the silent moments you spend with Him.

The quality of your spiritual life will be in direct proportion to the quality of your prayer life. So if you're enduring difficult times, do yourself a favor: Instead of turning things over in your mind, turn them over to God in prayer. Instead of worrying about your next decision, ask the Lord to lead the way. Don't limit your prayers to mealtimes or to bedtime. Pray constantly because God is listening, and He wants to hear from you. And without question, you need to hear from Him.

MORE THOUGHTS ABOUT PRAYER

Prayer wonderfully clears the vision; steadies the nerves; defines duty; stiffens the purpose; sweetens and strengthens the spirit.
S. D. GORDON

Prayer connects us with God's limitless potential.
HENRY BLACKABY

God shapes the world by prayer. The more praying there is in the world, the better the world will be, and the mightier will be the forces against evil.
E. M. BOUNDS

Prayer shouldn't be casual or sporadic, dictated only by the needs of the moment. Prayer should be as much a part of our lives as breathing.
BILLY GRAHAM

Prayer is the answer to every problem there is.
OSWALD CHAMBERS

MORE FROM GOD'S WORD

Anyone who is having troubles should pray.
JAMES 5:13 NCV

Don't worry about anything, but in everything, through prayer and petition with thanksgiving, let your requests be made known to God.
PHILIPPIANS 4:6 HCSB

Rejoice always, pray without ceasing, in everything give thanks; for this is the will of God in Christ Jesus for you.
1 THESSALONIANS 5:16–18 NKJV

REMEMBER THIS

Prayer is always necessary, but it's absolutely essential during difficult times. Martin Luther observed, "If I should neglect prayer but a single day, I should lose a great deal of the fire of faith." Those words apply to you too. And it's up to you to live—and to pray—accordingly.

A TIMELY TIP

If you need something, don't ask for God's help in general terms. Ask specifically for the things you need.

31

GOD CREATED YOU
FOR A SPECIFIC PURPOSE

WHAT THE BIBLE SAYS

For it is God who is working in you,
enabling you both to desire
and to work out His good purpose.

PHILIPPIANS 2:13 HCSB

What did God put me here to do?" If you're like most of people, you've asked yourself that question on many occasions. Perhaps you've pondered your future, uncertain of your plans, unsure of your next step. But even if you don't have a clear plan for the next step of your life's journey, you may rest assured that God does.

The Lord has a plan for the universe, and He has a plan for you. He understands that plan as thoroughly and completely as He knows you. If you seek God's will earnestly and prayerfully, He will make His plans known to you in His own time and in His own way.

Perhaps your vision of God's purpose for your life has been clouded by a wish list that you have expected God to dutifully fulfill. Perhaps you have fervently hoped that God would create a world that unfolds according to your wishes, not His. If so, you have experienced more disappointment than satisfaction and more frustration than peace. A better strategy is to conform your will to God's (and not to struggle vainly in an attempt to conform His will to yours).

Sometimes God's plans and purposes may seem unmistakably clear to you. If so, push ahead. But other times He may lead you through the wilderness before He directs you to the promised land. So be patient and keep seeking His will for your life. When you do, you'll be amazed at the marvelous things that an all-powerful, all-knowing God can do.

MORE THOUGHTS ABOUT DISCOVERING PURPOSE

You weren't an accident. You weren't mass produced. You aren't an assembly-line product. You were deliberately planned, specifically gifted, and lovingly positioned on the earth by the Master Craftsman.

MAX LUCADO

God meant for life to be filled with joy and purpose. He invites us to take our journey with Him.

BILLY GRAHAM

There's some task which the God of all the universe, the great Creator, has for you to do, and which will remain undone and incomplete, until by faith and obedience, you step into the will of God.

ALAN REDPATH

All of God's people are ordinary people who have been made extraordinary by the purpose He has given them.

OSWALD CHAMBERS

MORE FROM GOD'S WORD

For we are God's coworkers.
You are God's field, God's building.
1 Corinthians 3:9 HCSB

For we are His creation, created in
Christ Jesus for good works,
which God prepared ahead of time
so that we should walk in them.
Ephesians 2:10 HCSB

We must do the works of Him who
sent Me while it is day. Night is coming
when no one can work.
John 9:4 HCSB

REMEMBER THIS

God has big things in store for you, but He may have quite a few lessons to teach you before you are fully prepared to do His will and fulfill His purpose.

A TIMELY TIP

Perhaps you're in a hurry to understand God's unfolding plan for your life. If so, remember that God operates according to a perfect timetable. That timetable is His, not yours. So be patient.

32

WHEN YOU'RE EXPERIENCING TOUGH TIMES, KEEP WORKING

WHAT THE BIBLE SAYS

But this I say: He who sows sparingly will also reap sparingly, and he who sows bountifully will also reap bountifully.

2 CORINTHIANS 9:6 NKJV

The old adage is both familiar and true: We must pray as if everything depended upon God, but work as if everything depended upon us. Yet sometimes, when we are weary and discouraged, we may allow our worries to sap our energy and our hope. God has other intentions. God intends that we pray for things, and He intends that we be willing to work for the things that we pray for. More importantly, God intends that our work become His work.

God has created a world in which diligence is rewarded and sloth is not. So whatever you choose to do, do it with commitment, with excitement, with enthusiasm, and with vigor.

In his second letter to the Thessalonians, Paul warned, "If any would not work, neither should he eat" (3:10 KJV). And the book of Proverbs proclaims, "One who is slack in his work is brother to one who destroys" (18:9 NIV). Clearly, God's Word commends the value and importance of diligence. Yet we live in a world that, all too often, glorifies leisure while downplaying the importance of shoulder-to-the-wheel hard work. Rest assured, however, that God does not underestimate the value of diligence. And neither should you.

God did not create you to be ordinary; He created you for far greater things. Reaching for greater things usually requires work and lots of it, which is perfectly fine with God. After all, He knows that you're up to the task, and He has big plans for you. Very big plans.

MORE THOUGHTS ABOUT WORK

*Think of something you ought to do and go do it.
Heed not your feelings. Do your work.*
GEORGE MACDONALD

*When love and skill work together,
expect a masterpiece.*
JOHN RUSKIN

*All work, if offered to Him, is transformed. It is not
secular but sacred, sanctified in the glad offering.*
ELISABETH ELLIOT

*Ordinary work, which is what most of us do
most of the time, is ordained by God
every bit as much as is the extraordinary.*
ELISABETH ELLIOT

*It may be that the day of judgment will dawn
tomorrow; in that case, we shall gladly stop
working for a better future. But not before.*
DIETRICH BONHOEFFER

MORE FROM GOD'S WORD

Whatever you do, do it enthusiastically,
as something done for the Lord and not for men.
COLOSSIANS 3:23 HCSB

Be strong and courageous,
and do the work. Don't be afraid
or discouraged, for the LORD God,
my God, is with you. He won't
leave you or forsake you.
1 CHRONICLES 28:20 HCSB

I must work the works of Him who
sent Me while it is day; the night is coming
when no one can work.
JOHN 9:4 NKJV

REMEMBER THIS

You and God, working together, can accomplish great things for His kingdom. When you do your part, He will most certainly do His part.

A TIMELY TIP

Here's a time-tested formula for success: have faith in God and do the work. It has been said that there are no shortcuts to any place worth going. Hard work is not simply a proven way to get ahead, it's also part of God's plan for all His children (including you).

33

GOD GIVES STRENGTH

WHAT THE BIBLE SAYS

He gives strength to the weary, and to him
who lacks might He increases power.
Isaiah 40:29 NASB

Today, like every other day, is brimming with possibilities. Whether we realize it or not, the Lord is always working in us and through us; our job is to let Him do His work without undue interference. Yet we are imperfect beings who, because of our limited vision, often resist God's will. And oftentimes, because of our stubborn insistence on squeezing too many activities into a twenty-four-hour day, we allow ourselves to become exhausted, or frustrated, or both.

All of us must endure difficult days when our trust is tested and our strength is sapped. Thankfully, even on the darkest days, we need not endure our troubles alone. God's Word promises that He will renew our strength when we offer our hearts and prayers to Him.

The Bible promises that we can do all things through the power of our risen Savior, Jesus Christ. Our challenge, then, is clear: We must place Christ where he belongs: at the very center of our lives. When we do so, we will surely discover that He offers us the strength to live victoriously in this world and eternally in the next.

MORE THOUGHTS ABOUT STRENGTH

*A divine strength is given to those who yield
themselves to the Father and
obey what He tells them to do.*

WARREN WIERSBE

*Faith is a strong power, mastering
any difficulty in the strength of the Lord
who made heaven and earth.*

CORRIE TEN BOOM

*The resurrection of Jesus Christ is the power of God
to change history and to change lives.*

BILL BRIGHT

*God will give us the strength and resources
we need to live through any
situation in life that He ordains.*

BILLY GRAHAM

*Walking with God leads to receiving His intimate
counsel, and counseling leads to deep restoration.*

JOHN ELDREDGE

*Spending time with God is the key to our strength
and success in all areas of life. Be sure that you
never try to work God into your schedule,
but always work your schedule around Him.*

JOYCE MEYER

MORE FROM GOD'S WORD

The LORD is my strength and my song;
He has become my salvation.
EXODUS 15:2 HCSB

My grace is sufficient for you,
for my power is made perfect in weakness.
2 CORINTHIANS 12:9 NIV

Have faith in the LORD your God,
and you will stand strong.
Have faith in his prophets,
and you will succeed.
2 CHRONICLES 20:20 NCV

REMEMBER THIS

When you are fatigued, fearful, or discouraged, God can restore your strength. Your task, simply put, is to let Him.

A TIMELY TIP

Need strength? Let God's Spirit reign over your heart. And remember that the best time to begin living triumphantly is the present moment.

34

MAKE PEACE
WITH YOUR PAST

WHAT THE BIBLE SAYS

*Do not remember the former things, nor consider
the things of old. Behold, I will do a new thing.*
Isaiah 43:18–19 NKJV

The American theologian Reinhold Niebuhr composed a profoundly simple verse that came to be known as the Serenity Prayer: "God, grant me the serenity to accept the things I cannot change, the courage to change the things I can, and the wisdom to know the difference." Niebuhr's words are far easier to recite than they are to live by. Why? Because most of us want life to unfold in accordance with our own wishes and timetables. But sometimes God has other plans.

One of the things that fits nicely into the category of "things we cannot change" is the past. Yet even though we know that the past is unchangeable, many of us continue to invest energy worrying about the unfairness of yesterday (when we should, instead, be focusing on the opportunities of today and the promises of tomorrow).

Do you invest more time than you should reliving the past? Are you troubled by feelings of anger, bitterness, envy, or regret? Do you harbor ill will against someone you can't seem to forgive? If so, it's time to get serious about putting the past in its proper place: behind you.

Perhaps there's something in your past that you deeply regret.

Or maybe you've been scarred by a trauma that you simply can't seem to resolve. If so, it's time to ask for God's help—sincerely, prayerfully, and often—as you decide, once and for all, to move beyond yesterday's pain so you can more fully savor the precious present.

Of course, it's perfectly natural to fret over the injustices you've suffered and to hold grudges against the people who inflicted them. But God wants you to live in the present, not the past, and He knows that even when you can't forget, you can forgive and, by doing so, move on. It's the right thing to do and the right way to live.

MORE THOUGHTS ABOUT ACCEPTING THE PAST AND MOVING ON WITH LIFE

Finish every day and be done with it.
You have done what you could;
some blunders and absurdities have crept in;
forget them as soon as you can.

RALPH WALDO EMERSON

Our past experiences may have made us the way we are, but we don't have to stay that way.

JOYCE MEYER

Trust the past to God's mercy, the present to God's love, and the future to God's providence.

ST. AUGUSTINE

Don't be bound by the past and its failures.
But don't forget its lessons either.

BILLY GRAHAM

MORE FROM GOD'S WORD

*One thing I do, forgetting those things
which are behind and reaching forward
to those things which are ahead,
I press toward the goal for the prize
of the upward call of God in Christ Jesus.*
PHILIPPIANS 3:13–14 NKJV

*Your old sinful self has died,
and your new life is kept with Christ in God.*
COLOSSIANS 3:3 NCV

*And He who sits on the throne said,
"Behold, I am making all things new."*
REVELATION 21:5 NASB

REMEMBER THIS

The past is past, so don't live there. If you're focused on the past, change your focus. If you're living in the past, it's time to stop living there, starting now.

A TIMELY TIP

If you can't seem to stop focusing on the past, pray about it. When you ask God to heal your heart—and when you keep asking Him—He will help you accept your situation and move on.

35

STAY FOCUSED ON GOD'S GIFT OF ETERNAL LIFE

WHAT THE BIBLE SAYS

For God so loved the world, that he gave his only begotten Son, that whosoever believeth in him should not perish, but have everlasting life.

JOHN 3:16 KJV

Your life here on earth is merely a preparation for a far different life to come: the eternal life that God promises to those who welcome His Son into their hearts.

As a mere mortal, your vision for the future is finite. God's vision is not burdened by such limitations: His plans extend throughout all eternity. Thus, God's plans for you are not limited to the ups and downs of everyday life. Your heavenly Father has bigger things in mind . . . much bigger things.

How marvelous it is that God became a man and walked among us. Had He not chosen to do so, we might feel removed from a distant Creator. But ours is not a distant God. Ours is a God who understands—far better than we ever could—the essence of what it means to be human. God understands our hopes, our fears, and our temptations. He understands what it means to be angry and what it costs to forgive. He knows the heart, the conscience, and the soul of every person who has ever lived, including you.

As you struggle with the inevitable hardships and occasional disappointments of life here on earth, remember that God has invited you to accept His abundance not only for today but also for all eternity. So keep things in perspective. Although you will inevitably encounter occasional defeats in this world, you'll have all eternity to celebrate the ultimate victory in the next.

MORE THOUGHTS ABOUT ETERNAL LIFE

Jesus became mortal to give you immortality; and today, through Him, you can be free.

David Jeremiah

At most, you will live a hundred years on earth, but you will spend forever in eternity.

Rick Warren

Death is not a journey into an unknown land; it is a voyage home. We are going, not to a strange country, but to our Father's house.

John Ruskin

Everything that is joined to the immortal Head will share His immortality.

C. S. Lewis

You need to think more about eternity and not less.

Rick Warren

Death is not the end of life; it is only the gateway to eternity.

Billy Graham

MORE FROM GOD'S WORD

*I assure you: Anyone who hears
My word and believes Him who sent Me
has eternal life and will not come
under judgment but has
passed from death to life.*
JOHN 5:24 HCSB

*For the wages of sin is death,
but the gift of God is eternal life
in Christ Jesus our Lord.*
ROMANS 6:23 NIV

The last enemy that will be destroyed is death.
1 CORINTHIANS 15:26 NKJV

REMEMBER THIS

If you have already welcomed Christ into your heart as your personal Savior, then your eternal future is secure. If you're still sitting on the fence, the time to accept Him is this very moment.

A TIMELY TIP

Once you've welcomed Christ into your heart, you have an important story to tell: yours. So don't be hesitant to share your personal testimony with the world.

RECOGNIZING COMMON MOOD AND ANXIETY DISORDERS

Difficult times can be stressful. Very stressful. And when our stress levels are increased, we are at higher risk of experiencing a mood or anxiety disorder. These disorders can be serious, life-threatening conditions, but they're also highly treatable, so it's important to identify them early and to seek treatment expeditiously.

A mood disorder is a mental health condition that has an adverse effect on a person's emotional state. The two most common mood disorders are depression and bipolar disorder. Both of these conditions are further divided into subcategories based, in part, on the severity and duration of the person's symptoms.

An anxiety disorder is a condition that causes exaggerated emotions to interfere with a person's ability to lead a normal life. All of us feel anxious from time to time, but a person who experiences an anxiety disorder is faced with overwhelming, debilitating feelings of fear, dread, or panic. Obsessive behaviors—characterized by recurrent, unwanted thoughts (obsessions) or undesirable repetitive behaviors (compulsions)—are also considered to be anxiety-related conditions.

Mood and anxiety disorders are quite common. The National Institute of Mental Health (NIMH) estimates that almost 10 percent of US adults will experience a mood disorder during a given year and that over 20 percent of adults will experience a mood disorder sometime during their lifetime.

Anxiety disorders are even more common than mood disorders. In fact, the NIMH calls anxiety disorders "the most common mental health concern in the United States." They estimate that currently about 40 million adults (almost 20 percent of the adult population) suffer from some type of anxiety-related condition. Common anxiety disorders include, but are not limited to, generalized anxiety disorder, obsessive-compulsive disorder, panic disorder, post-traumatic stress disorder, and social anxiety disorder.

Both mood and anxiety disorders tend to run in families, which means that they can be inherited from one or both parents. Additionally, environmental factors—such as a traumatic event, a serious illness, or a significant life-changing situation—can be causal factors.

Clearly mood and anxiety disorders pose serious problems for individual sufferers and for the loved ones who care for them. Thankfully, these disorders are, in most cases, readily treatable with therapy or medication or a combination of the two, combined with self-care.

The following descriptions provide a brief introduction to the above-mentioned disorders. Should you need to learn more, detailed information is readily available. And if you suspect that you or someone you care about may be impacted by one of these disorders, or by a mental illness not mentioned here, don't wait to seek treatment. Mental health problems can evolve into serious, debilitating, life-threatening conditions. So it's always better to seek professional guidance sooner, rather than later.

THE MOST COMMON MOOD DISORDERS

Major Depression (also known as Major Depressive Disorder or Clinical Depression): Major depression is a common, serious mood disorder. It causes severe symptoms that affect how one feels, thinks, and manages daily activities such as sleeping, eating, or working. To be diagnosed with depression, symptoms must be present for at least two weeks. Symptoms include, but are not limited to:

- feelings of sadness, hopeless, or despondency
- feelings of guilt, worthlessness, or helplessness
- difficulty sleeping, early-morning awakening, or oversleeping
- having noticeably less interest in usual pleasurable activities
- decreased energy level
- appetite or weight changes
- feeling that life no longer has meaning
- irritability
- moving or talking more slowly
- feeling restless or having trouble sitting still
- difficulty concentrating, remembering, or making decisions
- thoughts of death or suicide, or suicide attempts
- aches or pains, headaches, cramps, or digestive problems that have no clear physical cause

Bipolar Disorder (also known as Manic-Depressive Disorder): According to NIMH, bipolar disorder is "a brain disorder that causes unusual shifts in mood, energy, activity levels, and the ability to carry out day-to-day tasks." People suffering with this condition experience episodes of depression alternating with periods of mania.

There are four basic types of bipolar disorder, all of which involve demonstrable changes in mood, energy, and activity levels. These moods vacillate between periods of extreme energy and/or irritability (known as manic episodes) followed by periods of extreme sadness, hopelessness, or despair (known as depressive episodes). According to NIMH, people experiencing manic episodes may exhibit some or most of the following symptoms:

- feeling very "up," "high," or elated

- feeling extremely energetic
- increased activity levels
- feeling jumpy or "wired"
- trouble falling asleep or staying asleep
- exhibiting pressured speech patterns, such as talking faster than normal
- feeling agitated, irritable, or "touchy"
- racing thoughts
- attempting to do many things at once

According to NIMH, bipolar patients experiencing depressive episodes may exhibit some or most of the following symptoms:

- feeling very sad, down, empty, or hopeless
- having very little energy
- exhibiting decreased activity levels
- trouble sleeping (either too little sleep or too much)
- feeling unable to enjoy anything
- feeling worried and empty
- trouble concentrating
- forgetfulness
- eating too much or too little
- feeling tired or "slowed down"
- thinking about death or suicide

OTHER COMMON MOOD DISORDERS

Persistent Depressive Disorder (also known as Dysthymia): This is a chronic, low-grade mood disorder in which symptoms of depression or irritability last for at least two years. A person diagnosed with persistent depressive disorder may experience episodes of major depression along with periods of less severe symptoms. But for a diagnosis of persistent depressive disorder, the depressive symptoms—both major symptoms and less severe ones—must last, in total, for at least two years.

Postpartum Depression: Many women become mildly depressed or anxious after the birth of a child. These symptoms, if they occur at all, typically clear within two weeks after delivery. Postpartum depression is a much more serious condition. Women with postpartum depression experience a full-blown major depression after delivery. Feelings of extreme sadness, anxiety, and exhaustion are common, thus making it difficult for mothers to care for themselves and for their babies.

Seasonal Affective Disorder (SAD): This is a form of depression that occurs during certain seasons of the year. Typically SAD begins in the late autumn or early winter and lasts until spring or summer. Less commonly, SAD episodes may begin during the late spring or summer. Symptoms of winter seasonal affective disorder often resemble those of major depression.

THE MOST COMMON ANXIETY DISORDERS

Generalized Anxiety Disorder (GAD): This condition is characterized by chronic anxiety, by exaggerated worry, tension, and apprehension even when there is no discernable cause for those feelings.

GAD, which often begins in the teen years or early adulthood, develops slowly. According to NIMH, symptoms of GAD include:
- being excessively worried about everyday things
- having trouble controlling worries or feelings of nervousness

- knowing that one's worries are exaggerated and excessive
- feeling restless; having trouble relaxing
- difficulty concentrating
- easily startled
- having trouble falling asleep or staying asleep
- feeling tired most or all the time
- experiencing physical symptoms, such as headaches, muscle aches, stomachaches, or unexplained pains
- difficulty swallowing
- experiencing twitches or tremors
- being irritable or feeling "on edge"
- sweating profusely, feeling lightheaded or out of breath

Children and teens with GAD often worry excessively about:

- performances in school, sports, or other public activities
- catastrophes such as earthquakes or wars

Adults with GAD are often highly nervous about everyday circumstances, such as:

- job security or performance
- health
- finances
- the health and well-being of their children
- being late
- completing household chores and other responsibilities

Post-traumatic Stress Disorder (PTSD): This disorder develops in some people who have either experienced or witnessed a terrifying, life-threatening, or life-altering event. PTSD symptoms may start within one month of the traumatic event, but for many individuals, symptoms may not appear until years later. These symptoms create significant problems in social settings, work-related environments, and relationships. PTSD symptoms are generally grouped into four categories: intrusive memories, avoidance, negative changes in thinking and mood, and changes in physical and emotional reactions.

Obsessive-Compulsive Disorder (OCD): This anxiety disorder is characterized by recurrent, unwanted thoughts (obsessions) and/or repetitive behaviors (compulsions). Repetitive behaviors such as hand washing, counting, checking, or cleaning are often performed with the hope of preventing obsessive thoughts or making those thoughts go away. Performing these rituals, however, provides only temporary relief. Not performing the aforementioned repetitive behaviors causes psychological discomfort and a marked increase in anxiety.

Panic Disorder: This anxiety disorder is characterized by unexpected and repeated episodes of intense fear (panic attacks) accompanied by physical and psychological symptoms that include:

- sudden and repeated panic attacks that result in overwhelming feelings of anxiety and fear
- the feeling of being out of control
- the fear of death or impending doom during a panic attack
- physical symptoms during a panic attack, such as a pounding or racing heart, sweating, chills, trembling, breathing problems, weakness or dizziness, tingly or numb hands, chest pain, stomach pain, or nausea
- an intense worry about when the next panic attack will occur
- a fear or avoidance of places where panic attacks have occurred in the past

Social Anxiety Disorder (also knowns as Social Phobia): This disorder is characterized by excessive self-consciousness and overwhelming anxiety resulting from social or performance situations in which the person is exposed to unfamiliar people or to possible scrutiny by others. A person with social phobia fears that he or she may act in a way—or may display anxiety-related symptoms—that will cause embarrassment or humiliation. In extreme cases, the phobia may be so broad that the sufferer experiences symptoms almost anytime he or she interacts with other people.

A FINAL NOTE

For previous generations, mental illness was often spoken about in whispers because, for many sufferers and their families, emotional disorders were a source of embarrassment or shame. Thankfully, this is no longer the case. Today, mental health is a top-of-mind priority for medical professionals who are keenly aware of countless studies that clearly demonstrate that most mental disorders have both physical as well as psychological origins. As such, most emotional disorders are now readily treatable. Thanks to advances in medical science, healing is available through counseling, through medication, or through a combination of the two.

If you suspect that you—or someone you care about—may be experiencing a mood disorder, an anxiety disorder, or any other psychiatric condition, don't hesitate to seek professional help. To fully experience God's abundance, you need to be spiritually and emotionally healthy. If mental health professionals can help you achieve the emotional stability you need to fully experience God's abundance here on earth, you should consider your treatment to be part of God's plan for your life.